DANGEROUS MEMORIES

Dangerous Memories

A Mosaic of Mary in Scripture

DRAWN FROM
Truly Our Sister

ELIZABETH A. JOHNSON

continuum
NEW YORK • LONDON

2004

The Continuum International Publishing Group Inc
15 East 26th Street, New York, NY 10017

The Continuum International Publishing Group Ltd
The Tower Building, 11 York Road, London SE1 7NX

www.continuumbooks.com

Library of Congress Cataloging-in-Publication Data

Johnson, Elizabeth A., 1941-
    [Dangerous memory of Mary]
    Dangerous memories : a mosaic of Mary in Scripture drawn from
Truly our sister / Elizabeth A. Johnson.
        p. cm.
    Originally published: Truly our sister, ch. 10, The dangerous memory
of Mary, ©2003. With new introd. and bibliography.
    Includes bibliographical references and index.
    ISBN 0-8264-1638-1 (pbk. : alk. paper)
    1. Mary, Blessed Virgin, Saint—Theology. 2. Catholic
Church—Doctrines. I. Title.
BT613.J65 2004
232.91—dc22

                                                    2004007759

In loving memory of
ANTHONY L. RUBSYS
(1923–2002)

priest, teacher, biblical scholar, translator,
lover of the world par excellence

"The learned will shine as brightly
as the vault of heaven, and those
who have instructed many in virtue,
as bright as stars for all eternity."
(Daniel 12:3)

Contents

Contents

Editor's Note

With a few minor changes, the bulk of *Dangerous Memories: A Mosaic of Mary in Scripture* is drawn from chapter 10, "The Dangerous Memory of Mary: A Mosaic," of *Truly Our Sister: A Theology of Mary in the Communion of Saints.* For the sake of economy, the 220 endnotes to chapter 10, pages 357–368, have been omitted. However, a bibliographic note at the back of this book acknowledges the principal works used as well as all the individual scholars mentioned in the notes. Anyone interested in finding the source for a particular nonbiblical quotation or for a particular idea is urged to consult *Truly Our Sister.*

Introduction

Finding Mary in the Worlds of the Text

WITH BEAUTIFUL ART, music, feast days, and prayers, every generation of Christians has honored Mary, the mother of Jesus. Because the child she bore is Emmanuel, God with us, this Jewish woman who lived in the first century is addressed with the profound title Mother of God. Her image adorns churches, schools, homes, and Christmas cribs, reminding people of the power and beauty of faith in Christ. The question before us today is this: How can our generation carry forward this rich, living tradition of honoring Mary? And what is the point of doing so? How can we, living in a multi-cultural church in the twenty-first century, appreciate Mary's significance for our life of faith and its practice?

This book traces one way. It proposes that we consider Mary as a woman of history, graced by the Spirit, who belongs now to the great "cloud of witnesses" whose lives challenge and inspire our own. It proposes that we connect with her as our companion in struggle, truly our sister in the communion of saints.

At the heart of this approach is a turn to scripture. There are more than a dozen stories in the New Testament where Mary appears, acts, or speaks. Reflecting the theology of the early church, these stories offer the possibility of retrieving her memory in a concrete way. Using contemporary methods of biblical study, we get glimpses of the world *behind* the biblical text—meaning the actual political, economic, religious, and cultural world that Miriam of Nazareth inhabited. We are also bathed in the world *of* the text, where her life is woven into the story of salvation coming from God in Jesus through the power of the Spirit. And we wrestle with the world *ahead* of the text, where, helped by this word of God, the faith community today strives to live faithfully and lovingly in our own time. These three worlds, behind, in, and in front of the scripture texts, interact to create a living memory of Mary that empowers the church. Together they form the framework for the reading of scripture in this book.

Behind the Text: The Woman of History

Our knowledge about the actual history of this woman is quite limited. At a minimum, we know that Miriam—for such was her name in Hebrew—was a Jewish woman, married and a mother, who lived in Galilee in the decades before and after the year "A.D. 1," by which the Western calendar now divides the eras. Thanks to contemporary scholarship, this small handful of facts opens a sizable window. Archaeological excavations, economic and sociological studies of the Roman empire, research on the role of women, and the study of ancient authors such as the Jewish historian Josephus, allow us to picture the world in which Miriam lived.

Start with her home in Nazareth, a small village in southern Galilee situated off the main road of commercial travel. Most of the hard remains that archaeology has uncovered here have to do with farming: olive presses, wine presses, cisterns for holding water, millstones for grinding grain, holes for storage jars. This indicates that the inhabitants, most likely numbering about three hundred to four hundred, were either peasants who worked their own land, tenant farmers who worked land belonging to others, or craftspersons who served their needs. Nothing that indicates wealth has been uncovered in Nazareth: no public paved roads or civic buildings, no inscriptions, no fresco decorations or mosaics, no luxury items such as perfume bottles or even simple glass.

The houses were small and clustered together. Each family occupied a domestic space or "house" of one or two small rooms built of native stone held together by a mortar of mud and smaller stones. Floors were made of packed earth. The roofs were thatched, constructed of thick bundles of reeds tied over beams of wood, most likely covered with packed mud for additional protection. Instead of standing alone, three or four of these small dwellings were clustered around a courtyard open to the sky. Surrounded by an outer stone wall, they formed a secure living space. The enclosed family rooms were used for sleep and sex, giving birth and dying, and taking shelter from the elements. In the unroofed, common courtyard, inhabitants of the domestic units, most likely an extended family or close kinship group, shared an oven, a cistern that held water, and a millstone for grinding grain—this was the kitchen where food was prepared and cooked in the open air. Domestic animals also lived here.

Alleyways or "streets" ran crookedly around the domestic enclosures in the village. One archaeologist, Jonathan Reed, notes that "none had channels for running water or sewage, which must have been tossed in the alleyways. Instead, the roads bend at the various clusters of houses, and were made of packed earth and dirt, dusty in the dry hot seasons and muddy in the short rainy seasons, but smelly throughout."[1] The people of the village shared larger food-preparation facilities such as a threshing floor, olive presses, and wine presses. Living at a subsistence level, inhabitants by and large grew their own food, did their own building, and sewed their own clothes from cloth that they spun and wove, mostly woolen cloth from sheep.

Miriam of Nazareth spent most of her adult life in this hamlet, most likely as part of an extended family, first as a married woman with her husband, Joseph, and then as a widow. In Palestine at this time, as indeed for most of human history, young people entered into marriages arranged by their families. According to contemporary Roman law, the minimum age of marriage for girls was twelve, for boys fourteen. Jewish practices were comparable, so that marriage for a girl usually took place at or just before puberty, usually between the ages of twelve and thirteen. This not only allowed maximum use of her childbearing years but also served her father's ability to guarantee her virginity, a heavy cultural and economic duty required by law.

According to Jewish custom, marriage was a process that took place in two stages. The first stage was the betrothal. This involved a formal exchange of the couple's consent to marry, made in the presence of witnesses and accompanied by the payment of the bride price from the bride's family to the groom. Unlike our culture's practice of getting engaged, betrothal constituted a legally ratified marriage even though the girl would remain in her own home for about one more year. After betrothal the two persons were henceforth husband and wife. The man had legal rights over the young woman. Any infringement of his marital sexual rights could be punished as adultery. Their union could be broken up only if he initiated a formal procedure of divorce. Betrothal also gave the girl the status of a married woman for many purposes. She was called the man's wife and could become his widow. The second stage occurred with the transfer of the young woman from her family home to her husband's family home, a formal move accompanied with some ceremony. He now assumed responsibility for her financial support, and they began to have sexual relations. Both Matthew and Luke reflect these marriage customs when they depict Mary's pregnancy beginning while she was betrothed to Joseph but "before they began to live together" (Matt 1:18), that is, before the second stage of their marriage took place. Knowing the baby wasn't his, Joseph initially decided to divorce Miriam. This made legitimate use of one of the options open to him—but notice that he was going to divorce her, not break their engagement: they were legally married.

A historical picture of Mary's Galilean household needs to account for the persons whom the gospels call Jesus' brothers and sisters. Mentioned in every gospel, in the Acts of the Apostles, and in some of Paul's letters, these family members were part of her world. The most extended entry comes in the scene where Jesus returns to his own village to teach in the synagogue on the sabbath. As Mark relates the event, many people of Nazareth took offense at him, wondering where he got all this wisdom. They said, "Is not this the carpenter, the son of Mary, and brother of James and Joses and Judas and Simon, and are not his sisters here among us?" (Mark 6:3). Matthew adapts the Markan version slightly to focus on Jesus' father's trade and seems to expand the number of sisters, having the villagers say, "Is not this the son of the carpenter? Is not his mother called Mary? And are not his brothers James and Joseph, Simon and Judas? And are not all his sisters here among us?" (Matt. 13:55-56).

Who are these four brothers and the multiple "all his sisters," unfortunately not named? Three positions existed in the early church, which correspond roughly to positions taken by

Christian churches today. (1) The brothers and sisters are the children of Mary and Joseph, born after the birth of Jesus, making them siblings in the usual sense. Aware that the perpetual virginity of Mary after the birth of Jesus is not a question raised directly by the New Testament, Protestant thinkers since the Enlightenment have generally tended to assume that this is the case. In this scenario, Jesus would be the oldest in a family of at least seven children: a large family with a small income. (2) The brothers and sisters are Joseph's children by a previous marriage. Appearing first in the apocryphal gospel of James in the mid-second century, this interpretation makes Mary their stepmother, with Jesus now the youngest of at least seven children. Widespread in the early church, this is still the favored explanation of Orthodox Christianity. (3) The brothers and sisters are actually Jesus' cousins. First championed by Jerome in the fourth century, this view has been adopted by the Roman Catholic Church and remains the official teaching of the church. This position is supported by the fact that the Greek term for blood brother, *adelphos*, can also mean relative, or member of the same clan or interest group. Contemporary biblical scholars point out, however, that there is a perfectly good Greek word for cousins that does appear elsewhere in the New Testament. Furthermore, all other passages that use "brother" or "sister" to describe family relationships use the terms in the sense of shared parentage rather than "cousins." Recall Zebedee's sons John and his brother James, the sisters Martha and Mary, their brother Lazarus, and Andrew with his brother Peter. Prescinding from faith and on purely historical and linguistic grounds, exegete John Meier judges that in the case of New Testament language about Jesus' relatives, "the most probable opinion is that the brothers and sisters of Jesus were true siblings." Other scholars such as John McHugh, however, defend the opinion that these children were born to Joseph's sister but brought up by Joseph after his brother-in-law died.

What is of interest here is the historical point that all three of the above interpretations, including the official Catholic "cousins" position, militate against Mary's mothering a one-child family. The manner in which the cousins, or four brothers and all the sisters, appear in Jesus' public life indicates relationships of long standing, leading scholars to think that these persons formed part of his family during his growing-up years. Even if these cousins did not live in the immediate household but perhaps shared a courtyard, their repeated presence yoked to the mother of Jesus in the gospels indicates a closeness of multiple children in this blended family. When these other children are taken into account, the romanticized picture of an ideal "holy family" composed of an old man, a young woman, and one perfect child needs to be revised.

In this setting, picturing this family's religious world turns us to first-century Judaism. An observant Jewish household, the family of Miriam lived out their faith through daily observance of the covenant laws, in sabbath rest and prayer, gatherings at synagogue, and, occasionally, in festival pilgrimages to the temple in Jerusalem. Historically speaking, it is important to remember that Mary's faith was not shaped by the devotion to Christ characteristic of later times once the gospels were written and doctrine developed. Nor is it adequate to say that Jewish belief and practice formed a mere "background" to her life. Loyal to the traditions of her ancestors, she inhabited this faith foursquare, bringing up her son Jesus in its beliefs and practices. To say that Mary lived and died a Jewish woman; that her religious gaze was focused on the God of Israel; that she shared the incipient christology of the early Jerusalem community rather than the high christology of Chalcedon; that she should not be depicted as having the piety of a latter-day Catholic, is not to demean her relationship with Jesus. It simply allows the deeply Jewish roots of her life and piety to be pictured in their actual historical integrity.

Nazareth was one of about two hundred small Jewish villages in southern Galilee. A province within the vast world of the Roman empire, Galilee was run as what scholars call a traditional agrarian society. The strongest characteristic of this kind of society was imbalance in material goods, with the labor of the poor majority, who worked the land, producing riches that flowed toward the wealthy governing minority, with little or no recompense. On one side were the ruler, his court and administrators, the military, merchants, and priests, who together comprised ten percent of the population. There was no middle class. On the other side of the money chasm was the peasant class, whose work on the land was the fundamental engine of the production of wealth. These people were supported by an artisan group made up of carpenters, metal tool makers, and other laborers, who most likely also worked their own plots of land. We need to guard against romantic images of the carpenter's shop. Being an artisan in a peasant society was much more economically precarious than being a skilled carpenter in an advanced, industrial market economy like our own.

At this time, Galilean villagers were triply taxed. In addition to the traditional tithe to support the temple and its priesthood in Jerusalem, they had to pay tribute to the Roman emperor, and yet more taxes to their local Jewish client-king, through whom Rome ruled by proxy (in Miriam's lifetime a string of Herods, father, son, and grandson, held this post). These tax monies were skimmed off as a certain percentage of the villagers' crops, flocks, or fish hauls.

The peasant communities worked intensely hard just to stay afloat, but the power of the governing class to extract payment ground them down. Drained of resources during these years, many fell into increasing indebtedness to the wealthy. As a result, they lost their land and became truly impoverished. The poverty and hunger in Galilee acted as a spawning ground for first-century revolts against the repressive Roman occupation and the taxation it engendered.

One incident not mentioned in the gospels but reported by Josephus illustrates this tension. Perched on a hill about four miles from Nazareth, the lovely city of Sepphoris was the administrative center in Galilee of the rule of King Herod the Great. He built it up and adorned it to be the tax collection headquarters for the whole region. When Herod died in 4 B.C., resentment exploded in revolt all over Palestine. Led by a peasant named Judas, a large band of desperate men attacked Sepphoris, raided the royal fortress, seized all the weapons stored there, and ransacked the city of all its goods. Facing widespread uproar, the Romans responded with brutal efficiency. In Jerusalem they crucified two thousand Jewish men outside the city walls. In Galilee they recaptured Sepphoris and, in Josephus's succinct summary, "burned the city and enslaved its inhabitants." Surrounding villages were leveled to punish the rebels among their inhabitants; people were sold into slavery. Historian Richard Horsley points out that, "in the villages around Sepphoris such as Nazareth, the people would have had vivid memories both of the outburst against Herod and the Romans, and of the destruction of their villages and the enslavement of their friends and relatives. . . . The mass enslavement and destruction would have left severe scars on the social body of the Galilean village communities for generations to come."[2]

Living in Nazareth at the time, Miriam would have been

around fifteen or sixteen years old, a young married woman with a new baby. She obviously survived the damage inflicted on her village by the rampaging Roman legions. Did she hide with other women in a cave in the Nazareth ridge as the tidal wave of violence went sweeping over? What terror, what loss from deaths, rapes, and looting had to be coped with? How much rebuilding absorbed their energy when psychically they were at a low ebb and materially they had so little to begin with? Sad to say, the wretched wars of the late twentieth and early twenty-first centuries, reported in the press and shown on television, leave little work for our imagination. Watching village women in Vietnam, El Salvador, Bosnia, East Timor, Congo, Afghanistan, and elsewhere flee, hide, be injured, all the while trying to protect their children, makes this picture all too real.

Married to the local village carpenter, Miriam of Nazareth lived in a world of social stratification marked by great disparities in wealth and privilege. Her life is typical of that of countless women throughout the ages who experience civic powerlessness, poverty, and the suffering that results from low status and lack of formal education. The ability to read and write was a relatively rare skill in the Greco-Roman world, a skill restricted largely to scribes and an intellectual elite. The vast majority of ordinary people were functionally illiterate, and so, most likely, was Miriam. Her social location also indicates that her physical appearance was not blond-haired, blue-eyed, and svelte. Along with the women of her class and ethnic heritage, she would have had Semitic features and Mediterranean coloring of skin, hair, and eyes. Commenting on how the ruling classes of medieval Europe and the Renaissance who patronized art and literature had turned the mother of Jesus into a upper-class, fair gentlewoman like themselves, "Our Lady," the pioneering biblical scholar John

L. McKenzie noted, "About Palestinian housewives they knew nothing. If they had, they would have found her like the maids of their palace kitchens or the peasant women of their domains."[3] Miriam of Nazareth occupied the lower rung of the social and economic ladder, and her life was lived out in an economically poor, politically oppressed, Jewish peasant culture marked by exploitation and publicly violent events.

Using the spade of archaeology, the measuring tools of social science, and the quill of ancient authors, we can picture the concrete world in which Mary lived. This picture is of interest not simply for historical reasons but also for religious ones. It intrigues us as the locus of Mary's encounter with God. It is precisely in this economic, political, and cultural setting, living out her Jewish faith as a peasant woman of the people, that Mary walked her journey of faith in response to the promptings of the Spirit. It is precisely to such a woman, who counts for nothing on the stage of world empire, that God has done great things. It is precisely such a woman who sings joyfully that God her Savior is coming to overturn oppression in favor of the poor of the earth. As we read the biblical stories, the circumstances pictured above come forward not as mere historical background but as the warp and woof of the world in which the revelation of God took place.

In the Text: Graced by the Spirit

The New Testament tells the story of salvation coming from God in Jesus through the power of the Spirit. As part of that story, it tells of individuals and groups who interacted with Jesus during his life, death, and resurrection. Miriam of Nazareth is one of these, receiving brief mention in each of the gospels. Written from a faith perspective, these texts connect her life to the grand, overarching narrative of the coming of salvation into the world. While they take the historical setting of her life for granted, they bring the story of grace to the fore. In Luke's view, for example, highly favored by God, blessed among women, called blessed by all generations, Mary heard the word of God and acted upon it. She is a woman graced by the Spirit.

The gospels never deny the humanity of Miriam of Nazareth or make it appear that she lived anything other than a regular human life with its joys and sufferings. In fact, during later controversies over the identity of Jesus Christ, the fact that his mother's pregnancy shaped his flesh from her own body became a critical argument defending his own genuine humanity. In later centuries, as Christians offered honor to Mary, they sometimes tended to glorify her to the point where her really human, historical life slipped from view. The doctrine of the Immaculate Conception in particular has had this effect, although this was not its intention. Declared in the nineteenth century, this doctrine holds that Mary herself was conceived without original sin. In the popular Catholic imagination, this seems to have effectively removed her from the human condition. She had, people say, special privileges that enabled her to cope with the troubles of life. Exempt from human passions, preserved from temptations, spared ambiguity when it came to decisions, always in full possession of her wits, clearly knowing God's plan for herself and her son and more than willing to carry it out, she moved through life with unearthly ease. The one allowable exception is the sorrow she felt at the cross, but even here, it is said, she willingly sacrificed her son for the redemption of the world. In this interpretation, Mary's conception without original sin dehumanizes her. She was perfect. Cocooned in a bubble, her humanity is bleached of blood and guts.

A way around this roadblock is found when we realize that being conceived without original sin does not mean being conceived in a vacuum. Rather, it means being uniquely blessed at the outset of life with the gift of grace. Let us think about this doctrine in the light of what sin and grace actually mean. They are opposites. Sin refers to the absence of God's life, grace to its presence. Theology today has shifted from the medieval focus on created grace, an extrinsic gift often pictured as a spiritual substance, to the more basic reality of uncreated grace, which is the radically precious gift of God's own self freely offered to persons. Uncreated grace is first and foremost God's self-communication and presence to human beings. In grace the mystery of the living, gracious God becomes present as the Spirit dwelling at the heart of human existence. In biblical terms, "the love of God has been poured into our hearts by the Holy Spirit who has been given to us" (Rom. 5:5). The "singular grace" that Mary, according to the doctrinal definition, received at her conception refers to what the church affirms to be God's self-gift, which is unfathomable. Put simply, Mary was enveloped from the beginning by the love of God. As one German name for the feast of the Immaculate Conception on December 8 puts it, this is "the feast of the be-gracing of Mary." The point is, while this doctrine speaks in the language of the absence of sin, in essence it is all about the presence of grace.

Now, what is the effect of grace on a human life? Does it make a person more human or does it dehumanize us? Does it protect us from struggle or give us a way through? The German theologian Karl Rahner offers a mind-teasing axiom that reveals a powerful answer: "nearness to God and genuine human autonomy grow in direct rather than inverse proportion."[4] In other words, God and the integrity of a person's human life are not in competition. Rather than diminish the wholeness of human life, grace enhances and fulfills it through union with the living God who is the goal of all creation including the human heart. Therefore, as Brazilian theologian Leonardo Boff explains, "To say that she is immaculate does not mean that she did not suffer, that she was never troubled, or that she had no need for faith and hope. She was a daughter of earth, albeit blessed by heaven. She had human passions. Everything authentically human was present in her."[5]

In light of this understanding of grace, Mary's original relationship to the Spirit creates her as a free, fully human being. She has to accomplish her life in the midst of the troubles of history, not angelically outside it. Plunged into the heart of the world, her life was a real human journey. She searched, she struggled, she had to compose her life as we all do. Thérèse of Lisieux pointed to this truth when she pondered why she loved Mary. It was not because the Mother of God received exceptional privileges, she wrote, blessings that would remove her from the ordinary condition, "ravishings, miracles, ecstasies," and the like, but because she lived and suffered simply, like us, in the dark night of faith.

To profess that Mary is graced in a special way is to affirm, then, in view of her vocation to be the woman through whom God became a child of earth, that God's personal self-communication in grace was given to this woman of the people from her beginning. Deep relationship to God did not erase her humanity. Firmly rooted in history, this first-century woman lived with all the limitations and difficulties that being human inevitably entails. Pope John Paul II's repeated references to Mary's own need for religious faith bear this out: her life was a pilgrimage of faith; she gave herself to God's word in the "dim light of faith"; like Abraham she had to "hope against hope"; though the mother of Christ, she was in contact with the mystery of his truth only through a "veil," having to be faithful even through the "night of faith."[6] In other words, even where it is most religiously crucial, she struggled through without extra advantages. Patricia Noone's humorous comment is particularly apt: Mary did not have the doctrine of the Immaculate Conception framed and hanging on her kitchen wall, assuring her that she was sinless and free from error.[7] Appreciating this historical slant, I would add that even if she did, it would not lift her feet off the ground. Understood as the living, self-communication of God's Spirit to Mary at the outset of her life, the Immaculate Conception does not extract her from the challenges that come with life on this planet. Rather, in its peculiar, time-conditioned way, it fundamentally asserts the living God's self-gift to this woman who is called to a special vocation in salvation history. In so doing, it signals that when it comes to God's intent, grace is more original than sin.

Linking this understanding of the graced woman in the biblical texts with the historical woman behind the texts yields a powerful insight. It reveals that the light of God shines on persons who are regarded as insignificant in this world. Brazilian theologians Ivone Gebara and María Clara Bingemer point out that the *Immaculata* venerated on our altars is the same Miriam of Nazareth who was marginalized by the social structure of her time. To understand the doctrine aright, we cannot forget that it talks of God's exalting a woman who lived in poverty and anonymity, like millions of poor people today. This Galilean villager bears within herself the confirmation of God's preference for what is poor, small, and unprotected in this world. Adhering to this doctrine means proclaiming that the woman who gave birth in a stable among animals, who shared a life of poverty, who stood at the foot of the cross as the mother of the condemned, has been chosen by God. This sparks hope in the poor and oppressed and in those who stand in solidarity with them that they too will share in the blessings of the incarnate God.[8]

Ahead of the Text: Companion in the Communion of Saints

The historical world behind the text and the religious world of the text both interact in the faith world ahead of the text, our own world here and now. This is where the Christian community of today endeavors to live faithfully and lovingly according to the gospel message. As part of this ongoing process, the church honors numerous holy people, including Mary, the mother of Jesus. The memory of her partnership with God can challenge, console, and create liberating energies for life in the church and the world. What is the dynamic basis of the connection between her past and our present? It is the relationship known as the communion of saints.

Down through the centuries, as the Holy Spirit graces person after person in land after land, they form together a grand company of women and men brushed with the fire of divine love, a community of redeemed sinners. This is a multigenerational community of graced persons alive at any moment that geographically encircles the globe. It also stretches historically backward and forward in time to include those who have died and now live in the embrace of God. This community is a most inclusive group. It crosses boundaries of language, culture, race, sex, class, sexual orientation, religion, and all other human differences, stretching into eternity. The inmost depth and outermost horizon of this community of holy people remains God's Holy Spirit, who vivifies creation, weaves unifying connections, saves what is lost, and makes holy the world. This is the way to think about the communion of saints: it refers to the great and diverse multitude of people who are connected to God and one another through the Spirit's gift of grace.

A rich metaphor in the biblical book of Wisdom introduces fresh vocabulary for this communion. All through this book the female figure of Wisdom (Sophia in the original Greek) operates as an image of God actively creating and saving the world. In one passage, Wisdom's work is described this way:

> Although she is but one, she can do all things,
> and while remaining in herself, she renews all things;
> in every generation she passes into holy souls
> and makes them friends of God, and prophets.
>
> (Wis. 7.27)

• To be a friend of God is to enter into a relationship of affection with God, freely, with trust; taking time to savor the relationship in prayer and contemplation; allowing divine presence to be the foundation of your life even when it is experienced as wrenching absence.

• To be a prophet is to raise your voice in criticism against injustice because, being God's friend, you love the world in your heart the way God does; your imagination sees how it should flourish; when this collides with suffering, you are moved to console the oppressed and confront the powerful, thus creating possibilities for resistance and resurrection.

As a first-century Jewish woman of faith who responded full-heartedly to the Spirit, Mary is a friend of God and prophet who belongs in this company of grace. Living out her vocation in her own time and place, she is linked to all who respond to the gift of the Spirit in their own lives, in ways seen and unseen. In no way does this placement among the friends of God and prophets diminish her unique historic vocation to be the mother of the Messiah. But while honoring this pivotal relationship, it refocuses her significance for the community today in terms of her whole graced life lived before God.

Reading the biblical stories about Mary releases the power of her life into the world ahead of the text, especially if we relate to her as a companion. Traditionally, pious practices and preaching presented Mary and the other saints as patrons to our needs. We approached them primarily as intercessors before the throne of God. Being far from this distant throne, we ordinary people need more important persons to plead our cause and obtain blessings. We need friends in high places, so to speak. Because she is the Mother of the Lord, Mary is the most powerful intercessor of all, obtaining gifts that might otherwise be denied. This patron–client relationship is not found in the New Testament nor in the early Christian centuries. It developed in the late Roman empire under the influence of the civil patronage system once the church had been officially established.

A very different pattern of relationship is found in the New Testament and the age of the early martyrs. This model promotes companionship in Christ between the living and the dead. The living members of the church understand themselves to be on a journey that the friends of God and prophets in heaven have already completed. The two become partners, companions, comrades, and co-disciples in the life

of faith. Those who have died give their witness; those struggling to live faithfully on earth remember them; and both are
encompassed by the saving grace of God. Here Mary and the
saints in heaven stand not *between* God and those on earth,
but *alongside* their sisters and brothers in the one Spirit-filled
community. The letter to the Hebrews envisions it this way:
these ancestors in the faith are a great "cloud of witnesses"
(Heb. 12:1) who surround us with the encouragement of
their lives. At one time they were down on the track running
the race, but now they are up in the stands cheering us on.
Surrounded by this cloud of witnesses, we cherish in very different circumstances what they cared enough to live and die
for. As Augustine preached, "We marvel at them, they have
compassion on us. . . . Yet do we all serve one Lord, follow one
teacher, attend one king. We are all joined to one head, journey to the same Jerusalem, follow after the one love."

In the companionship relationship, one core practice that
connects living persons with those who have died is the act of
remembering. This is not a sentimental remembering that
bathes the past in a rosy glow. Rather, it recalls the courage,
suffering, wisdom, beauty, defeats, and victories of people
who struggled before us in order to unlock what Augustine
calls their "lessons of encouragement." This is memory with
the seed of the future in it. By bringing the witness of past
lives forward into the present, it connects us with their unfin-
ished agenda, shows that something more is possible, and
bolsters our own commitment.

In a provocative turn of phrase, the German theologian
Johannes Baptist Metz has called this kind of remembering
dangerous. Why dangerous? Because it interrupts the present
moment, which can be all-absorbing, and discloses that
something more is possible. If the times are fat and comfort-

able, it calls our present complacency into question, saying: there is more to life than the acquisition of things and the search for the latest entertainment. If the times are lean and tough, it calls our present affliction into question, saying: take heart; the powerful will not always win; God is in solidarity with you promising salvation. In situations of injustice, it challenges the status quo, saying: you can resist the course of things. By bringing "something more" into view, it reminds us of a future worth struggling for and sets our feet on the path of active discipleship. Remembering the saints this way creates a moral and social force that propels the church out of passivity into active engagement on behalf of all those in agony. It has a transforming power that energizes resistance and active love. In the light of their dangerous memory, we become partners in hope.

Remembering Miriam of Nazareth in this vein can be dangerous to both complacency and despair. Connecting her multifaceted story with our own releases transformative power in our lives. Hearing the word of God and keeping it, she actively partnered the divine work of repairing the world. While the precise circumstances of her actual life can never be repeated, the style and spirit of her life reverberate through the centuries to propel us forward in today's different cultural contexts. In solidarity with her in the one company of God's friends and prophets, we find strength to face up to our own encounters with the Spirit and to go forward with the best of our faithful wits. This impetus receives a critical edge when we remember Mary as poor, female, and endangered in a violent society. Then the vital memory of this woman of Spirit has the quality of "danger" insofar as it births wisdom, awakens resistance, and inspires active hope for a just and peaceful world in which poor people, women, indeed all human beings and the earth, can flourish as beloved of God.

Crafting a Mosaic

Keeping the worlds behind, in, and ahead of the text in view, this book turns to scripture as a primary resource for the dangerous memory of Mary. Composed over many decades after Pentecost, the books of the New Testament bear the early church's witness to what God has done in Jesus Christ for the salvation of the world. Rooted in history, these are profoundly theological writings. In a handful of brief episodes Miriam of Nazareth, identified either by her own name or as the mother of Jesus, speaks, takes action, or is described as an essential part of the action. Matthew and Luke place her primarily at the beginning of Jesus' life; John depicts her at the end by the cross; all four gospels have scenarios where she appears during the public ministry; Luke takes the further step of naming her among the women and men disciples of Jesus in the upper room before Pentecost. In probing these scenes for the memory of Mary they carry, this book employs two types of biblical scholarship as primary tools. The first, historical criticism, attempts to sort out literary genres and layers of composition of the texts, thereby clarifying original events from the religious explanations of the gospel writers. The second, feminist criticism, interprets texts through the eyes of women, seeking out what enhances or disparages women's human dignity.

1. Historical criticism holds a fairly solid though not undisputed consensus that the four canonical gospels came into being in three stages, starting with the life, death, and resurrection of Jesus of Nazareth witnessed by his disciples, moving next to the oral preaching of the early church, and peaking with the actual writing of the gospels by the evangelists in view of the needs of their churches. While there is some

dispute about chronology, a fairly broad agreement also exists that Mark wrote first in the seventies; a decade or so later Matthew and Luke adapted his work, adding sayings of Jesus from a common source (Q) along with their own diverse materials; and John composed last, toward the end of the first century, using his own original sources. Since most of the marian material appears in the first two chapters of Matthew and Luke, the literary genre of infancy narrative comes in for special attention. Obviously there were no apostolic eyewitnesses to the events of Jesus' conception and birth, nor did these events enter into the early preaching of the church, which focused on the paschal mystery. The provenance of these infancy stories is a skein of small strands of oral tradition, colored by pigment from birth stories in the Hebrew Scriptures, which the evangelists wove into imaginative, theologically powerful scenes that proclaim the identity and mission of Jesus the Christ. Composing these narratives last, after the main body of their gospels had been written, but placing them first, Matthew and Luke in effect created christological overtures that sound all the themes that will show up later in their gospels.

One of the major achievements of modern biblical scholarship is the clarity with which it emphasizes that these gospels are all faith documents. All four gospels have as their purpose to announce the good news of salvation coming from God in Jesus through the power of the Spirit, and to bring this story to bear on the spiritual and practical needs of a particular community of believers. Their intent is not flat-out historical or biographical but missionary and community building: to provide the church with witness to God's gracious mercy in Jesus and to provide guidance for walking in the "Way" according to the Spirit. Consequently, all the gospel writers read the post-resurrection situation back into the ministry and birth of Jesus, interpreting the traditions they received about his words and deeds in light of what they now knew to be the marvelous, God-given outcome of the story of his defeat. They chose certain memories, omitted others, paraphrased his words, and interpreted his healings, inclusive table companionship, and conflicts so as to grapple with the meaning of his identity and mission. Knowing that post-Easter faith in Jesus as Messiah, Lord, and Savior shaped the gospels' presentations, as did the current challenges and conflicts faced by the different local churches which were the intended audience, biblical scholarship encourages an appreciative approach to their diversity. Rather than trying to harmonize their different theological perspectives, we need to understand that each one's voice is important.

Traditional mariology achieved a synthesized view of Mary by harmonizing the diverse gospel texts into a smooth-running narrative of her life. New methods bring new results. Departing from centuries of literal exegesis, we now know that we cannot write a historical biography or psychological study of Mary. In place of such a unifying schema, we acknowledge and honor the fact that the gospels have distinctly different views about Mary because of the evangelists' diverse theologies. Drawing on these various gospel portraits, consequently, does not produce material for a complete biography but gives different glimpses, snapshots, vignettes, or brief portrayals of incidents in her life in scenes that are part of each gospel's testimony of faith in God.

2. The field of feminist interpretation, working with these standard biblical methods, raises the further, critical question of gender bias in both composition and interpretation of texts. The gospels, while part of inspired scripture in the church, are also marked by the sin of the society in which they were crafted, including acceptance of slavery, violence, and

patriarchy. They were written by educated men who apparently did not suffer directly from these abuses and whose work tends to erase the experience of those who did. Recall the classic statement in Matthew's account of Jesus feeding the multitudes. The story concludes: "And those who ate were about five thousand men, not counting women and children" (Matt. 14:21). Surely this is not because their appetites were so small as to be unworthy of mention, but because their persons were unimportant. In the worldview of the ruling men, such persons literally did not count. This pattern holds true throughout the Bible. The presence and creative activity of women are consistently omitted, played down, or criticized by the patriarchal orientation of the authors. We read these texts, furthermore, through a history of translation, commentary, and preaching shaped by the clerical culture of the church that has given rise to various interpretations that are oppressive to women but which women resist today, including the picture of Mary as a passive, silent, obedient handmaid.

To free up the word of God, a wide variety of methods come into play. Making the strategic move of placing women's personal and political experience at the center of attention, these methods suspect, critically evaluate, correct, historically reconstruct, and creatively imagine the silenced, marginalized women buried in the text along with the prejudicial theories that put them there. They aim to uncover possibilities for changing relations of domination inscribed in the text and in everyday life, being particularly accountable to women who struggle at the bottom of the pyramid of discrimination. Like the woman of the gospel looking for her lost coin, these methods search diligently "for submerged meanings, lost voices, and authorizing visions"[9] that will inspire religious imagination for a different, more mutual future for women and men together.

Using these methods opens up new readings of the stories of Mary in scripture. I suggest that the work of crafting a mosaic provides a useful metaphor for the work that lies ahead. Unlike a coherent sweep of line that shapes a traditional painting, a mosaic is made up of small fragments of colored stone or marble, called tesserae in the language of art. Each sliver alone is no more than a spot of color. Working according to a pattern, artists inlay these chips in plaster or cement. Assembled together they display a picture or an intelligent design, ever more clearly the farther back you stand. But it is always possible to move in again and see the individual bits of stone.

Like chips of a great mosaic, the marian texts of scripture are distinct images that do not form a complete picture on their own. They are glued into the story of Jesus Christ, which itself presumes the whole biblical sweep of God's gracious history with the world. We study these tesserae, these individual theological memories of Mary, as flashes of color that form part of the texture of the story of the living God's engagement with the history of the world. Allowing the three worlds of the text to interact, we shape a living memory of Miriam of Nazareth. Closer up, assembled together, the individual biblical stories form an image of a woman of Spirit. Honed by the historical background of Galilean Judaism and interpreted by women's experiences of the Spirit of God in different global locations, this mosaic delivers a glimpse of an actual woman, a first-century member of an oppressed peasant society, who partnered God in the great work of redemption.

To sum up: scripture provides us with a mosaic of Mary, the historical, graced, human woman, that allows us to remember her as our companion in the company of friends of God and prophets. Entirely particular, lived out within the constraints of first-century patriarchal society, her life with its concrete details in no way functions as culturally normative for women's lives today, lives racing along in a world she never dreamed of. But the dangerous memory of her partnership with God through the power of the Spirit can create liberating energies for the life of discipleship today. In all her difference, Miriam of Nazareth abides in the circle of disciples as our sister, a poor woman of the people to whom God has done great things; a God-bearer who had divinity dancing under her heart in developing human flesh; a young Jewish woman vulnerable to violence in a patriarchal setting; a friend of God who made her own difficult choices with courage; a prophet whose word announced the awesome reversals God's coming will bring about in this world; a married woman who toiled hard with her husband to provide for their family; a woman with a questioning mind who pondered what God was doing in the midst of her life; the mother of the itinerant preacher Jesus terribly worried about his ministry; a middle-aged woman whose agonized grief over the public execution of her firstborn connects her with legions of bereaved women; an elder in the budding community of the early church. She kept faith. We remember her. We connect her Spirit-filled story with our own amid the drama of the human race in its history of suffering and hope. We thereby find courage to carry forward God's dream for the world. The dangerous memory of Mary crafts a theology capable of promoting action on behalf of global justice and peace, particularly empowering to the flourishing of women, coherent with elements of biblical, classical, and conciliar church teaching, and productive of religious meaning for our time.

Notes

1. Jonathan L. Reed, *Archaeology and the Galilean Jesus: A Re-examination of the Evidence* (Harrisburg, Pa.: Trinity Press International, 2000), 153.

2. Richard A. Horsley, *Archaeology, History, and Society in Galilee: The Social Context of Jesus and the Rabbis* (Harrisburg, Pa.: Trinity Press International, 1996), 32 and 112.

3. John L. McKenzie, "The Mother of Jesus in the New Testament," in *Mary in the Churches*, ed. Hans Küng and Jürgen Moltmann (Edinburgh: T & T Clark; New York: Seabury, 1985), 9.

4. Karl Rahner, *Foundations of Christian Faith: An Introduction to the Idea of Christianity* (New York: Seabury, 1978), 226.

5. Leonardo Boff, *The Maternal Face of God: The Feminine and Its Religious Expressions* (Maryknoll, N.Y.: Orbis, 1987), 130.

6. John Paul II, encyclical *Redemptoris Mater*, in *Origins* 16:43 (April 9, 1987), par. 14 and 17.

7. Patricia Noone, *Mary for Today* (Chicago: Thomas More Press, 1977), 62.

8. Ivone Gebara and Maria Clara Bingemer, *Mary, Mother of God, Mother of the Poor* (Maryknoll, N.Y.: Orbis, 1989), 113.

9. See Elisabeth Schüssler Fiorenza, *Wisdom Ways: Introducing Feminist Biblical Interpretation* (Maryknoll, N.Y.: Orbis, 2001).

Outside

Mark 3:20–21 and 31–35

THE FIRST TESSERA for this marian mosaic comes from the earliest gospel, Mark. The story is set in the lake village of Capernaum, where Jesus has begun a ministry of preaching and healing that is drawing large, enthusiastic crowds. Hearing of this, "his own," also translated as his family or his relatives, set out to seize him and bring him home to Nazareth because they think he has lost his mind. Mark fills in the time it takes for them to arrive with a hostile exchange between Jesus and some scribes from Jerusalem, who accuse him of being in league with Satan. As that dispute winds down, Jesus is told that his family has arrived: "your mother and your brothers are outside, asking for you." Tension fills the air. Instead of rising at once and greeting them as custom and law requires, he emphatically "rejects," "repudiates," "disowns" his family using characteristic Jewish dialogue: Who are they?

> "Who are my mother and my brothers?" And looking around on those who sat about him, he said, "Here are my mother and my brothers. Whoever does the will of God is brother and sister and mother to me."

Jesus' words are rife with new vision. Blood ties do not guarantee a place in his community of disciples, but loving and acting on behalf of the reign of God do. The blessedness he offers is open to anyone who wants it, without distinction of sex or gender, infertility or maternity, physical kinship or family connections, so long as they seek the will of God. As Mark structures it, the scene draws a strong contrast between Jesus' biological family and a new kind of inclusive community, the eschatological family called into being by shared commitment to doing the will of God. According to this criterion, the mother and brothers of this popular preacher-healer stand outside, not inside with his disciples. Jesus "emphatically distances himself from his blood family." In their stead, "looking around on those who sat about him," he visually and verbally embraces the people in the house, who, unlike his family, do not think he is beside himself nor possessed of a demon. These are his true kin, the authentic family of God. They replace his natural family in importance.

Biblical scholar Joanna Dewey points out that Jesus' redefinition of kinship "is extremely radical in its first-century context," especially for women. The eschatological family depicted here is not patriarchal, not ruled by or even defined by a male head of household. There are no fathers. Even Jesus himself does not assume patriarchal authority but interprets himself as a brother and a son to all in the group. Women are redefined as his sisters and mother. In place of obedience to husband and father, they owe fidelity only to God in a community built up not by subservience but by nurturing and collegial relationships. In this context Mark's gospel goes on to depict a cast of strong women who interact dynamically with Jesus in ways that benefit themselves and also challenge and change him. Consider the Syro-Phoenician woman, fighting for her daughter, who teaches this Jewish prophet to think more inclusively about his mission (Mark 7:24–30); the unnamed woman who prophetically anoints his living body for burial, receiving the encomium that "wherever the gospel is preached in the whole world, what she has done will be told in memory of her" (Mark 14:3–9); and the women disciples from Galilee whom the gospel describes during the passion as looking on, watching, and seeing—classic verbs describing those who bear witness (Mark 15:40, 47). By contrast, the mother of Jesus here is a foil for authentic discipleship.

This negative portrait is strengthened by a later Markan scene that depicts Jesus' rejection when he does go back to preach in his home village of Nazareth. Responding to the neighbors who take offense at him, the son of Mary says, "A prophet is not without honor except in his own country and among his own kin and in his own house" (Mark 6:4). The scene gives support to the contention that Jesus' own natural family neither understood nor honored him, a tradition that, even though Mark emphasizes it the most, appears also in other gospels. These family tensions and Jesus' sharp disengagement from his mother and brothers during his ministry have good claim to a historical root. Remembering that after Easter Mary shared the faith of the earliest Christian community, the ecumenical team of *Mary in the New Testament* reasons that "since she was from the first a member of the post-Easter community, it is unlikely that her earlier misunderstanding of her Son is simply a creation of Mark or of the tradition he repeats; for it is hard to believe that such a misunderstanding would have been attributed to the believing mother of the risen Lord if there had been no basis for such an attribution. The basis seems to have been that, in fact, she did not follow Jesus about as a disciple during the ministry."

It is instructive to watch how Matthew and Luke edit this scene according to their own interests. Toning down the rejection a bit, Matthew omits the information that Jesus' family has come to seize him because they think he is beside himself. They just show up. However, Matthew still describes a strong contrast between natural family and disciples in Jesus' rhetoric and gesture: "Who is my mother and who are my brothers? And stretching out his hand toward his disciples, he said, Here are my mother and my brothers . . ." [Matt. 12:46–50]). By contrast, Luke shifts the whole event into a positive mode (8:19–20). Not only does he too omit the damaging information about the family's motivation for their trip, but by omitting the question "Who are my mother and my brothers?" and the replacement answer "Here are my mother and brothers," he drops the outside–inside contrast. While the criterion for belonging to the community of disciples is the same, namely, hearing the word of God and acting upon it, Jesus' mother and brothers now meet that criterion. Any implication that the family is hostile or does not understand is avoided. Instead, they are counted among the disciples. Biblical scholars desiring to defend the good name of Jesus' family point out that there is nothing in Mark's original scenario that would *prevent* mother and brothers from becoming part of the eschatological family, *eventually*. Still, in the Markan account they are clearly "outside."

Traditional mariology that glorified Mary never knew what to do with this text and as a consequence largely ignored it. In my judgment, it is an irreplaceable antidote to distortions of the tradition as well as a contribution to the memory of Mary in its own right. Here Jesus' mother and brothers arrive as a family and are disowned together. Whether these boys are her natural children, stepchildren, or nephews, their close association in this crisis places her in maternal relationship to more than one child. Here, too, the relationship between mother and her firstborn son is strained, pouring cold water on the multitude of traditional sentimental reflections about Jesus' relationship with his mother. Psychologically, to reach maturity men cannot stay fixated on their mother but must move out to form relationships within their own peer group. We see a healthy development in this episode.

A feminist interpretation does not seek to change Jesus' critical attitude toward his family, but sees Mary in a different light. Standard commentaries on this passage hold that at the very least Jesus' mother and brothers misunderstood him. Perhaps they did, this being an instance of a truly gifted person soaring beyond the vision and expectations of a typical family. It might just as well be the case, though, that they understood him only too well and sought to forestall what they saw as inevitably disastrous consequences. Parents whose children take risks to follow their dream in dangerous situations know the feelings well: the fear, the pride, the effort to protect. In Miriam of Nazareth's case, as one Jewish writer observes, "This son . . . roams around through the country and creates unrest. He does things that are dangerous: danger threatens from the Jewish authorities and from the hated occupying power of the Romans. He puts *the whole family at risk*." Making this trip, the unnamed mother of Jesus gives the lie to passive obedience as the key to her nature. Who better to have organized such a family expedition? In response to his behavior, which not only "rejected village norms for eldest sons" but also opened the door to disaster for himself and his kin, she and his brothers took action that they considered to be for his own good. They set out to fetch him home. Propelled by the Spirit to follow his own calling, however, Jesus meets their initiative with his own. He moves on without them.

In her feminist analysis of evil, ethicist Nel Noddings criticizes classical notions of evil that have equated it with sinful disobedience to the patriarch and his representatives, human and divine. Such an understanding, she argues, is not adequate to women's experiences. When women are consulted, it becomes clear that evil is defined as that which harms or threatens to harm them and those they love. Chief among the basic evils, considered phenomenologically, that women experience are useless, intractable pain along with the failure to alleviate it; separation or neglect of relation; and helplessness along with the mystification that sustains it. By contrast, moral good and the virtues that promote it are best expressed in an ethic of care that gives powerful impetus to building and remaining in loving relations. Continuing this kind of analysis, Sara Ruddick points to three great interests that govern the actions of those who mother the young: preserving the life of the child, fostering its growth, and shaping an acceptable child. Rather than follow the dictates of law and society were these to threaten the young, maternal thinking issues in ethical action to preserve and protect, regardless. In this light, a feminist perspective espies the exercise of female power in the action of Miriam of Nazareth, who, no stranger to Roman violence and the havoc it could wreak on human lives, goes to persuade her child out of the line of fire. I am reminded of an essay in the *New Yorker* after John F. Kennedy Jr. died along with his wife and her sister while piloting a small aircraft. While she lived, Jacqueline Kennedy Onassis disapproved of her son's wish to fly. The lessons, the license, and the new plane arrived only after her death. Moved by sorrow and aggravation at the loss of these promising young lives, the essayist wants to scream on the wind: *Listen to your mother!*

My point is not to undo or reconfigure the events that Christians believe brought about salvation, central to which are the miserable death and surprising resurrection of Jesus the Christ. A whole new appreciative belief in God-for-us welled up historically out of those events. What happened,

happened, and in the end we call it grace. In retrieving this Markan scene as a valuable chip for the memory mosaic of Mary, however, we gain a glimpse of a moment in time before these events took place. Full of concern for one she loves, Miriam of Nazareth does not have the New Testament to help her interpret God's designs. Embarking on a mission that ultimately fails, she stands "outside" with an anxious mind and heart, the frustrated, angry mother of Elisabeth Moltmann-Wendel's image, maladapted to the shedding of blood. We should be wary about judging this scene as evidence of lack of faith. The scholars of *Mary in the New Testament* rather sweepingly declare that the event behind this scene took place *before* "the time at which Mary's belief began," by which they mean more precisely the post-resurrection understanding of Jesus that she shared with the Jerusalem community. While this may be true in a Christian sense, her faith in God did not begin only after Easter, as witnessed by this scene, where her faith is at full pitch. Believing in God, Creator and Redeemer of the world, this Jewish woman partners the divine work of love by seeking to preserve and protect a precious life. No submissive handmaid, her memory moves in solidarity with women everywhere who act critically according to their best lights to seek the well-being of those they love.

In the Company of the Unconventional Foremothers ෫

Matthew 1:1–17

TURNING TO MATTHEW'S GOSPEL, we find that the infancy narrative that forms the first two chapters offers four new tesserae for the marian mosaic. The first stone is the genealogy that opens the gospel. This list of ancestors traces Jesus' lineage from Abraham through King David down to Joseph, "the husband of Mary, of whom was begotten Jesus, who is called the Messiah." Locating Jesus deep within the Jewish tradition, it has the purpose of introducing him as the fulfillment of messianic hopes. When this text is read in liturgical assembly, eyes tend to glaze over with the repetition of the "begats," A was the father of B, B was the father of C, and so on, with the heritage passed on by men of mostly unpronounceable names. Raymond Brown proposes the captivating idea that the church needs to read this text during Advent to remind ourselves that just as most of these people were ordinary folk who nevertheless advanced God's plan, so too ordinary people in the church today can contribute to God's coming into the world by fidelity in the midst of everyday life.

In view of seeking the memory of Mary, there is an even more interesting aspect to consider. This genealogy is terribly androcentric, with the lineage passing down through the fathers in orderly progression. The women who did the work of bearing the sons of each generation go largely unnamed, hidden by the patriarchal construct that considers women only vehicles of reproduction rather than historical agents in their own right. Even Mary is subsumed into Joseph's story in this manner. In Matthew's rendering she neither speaks, nor receives divine revelation, nor expresses a point of view. Yet this overall androcentric pattern of history breaks open when the genealogy lists four female ancestors by name and goes on even more dramatically to change the paternity pattern in Mary's case. In Elaine Wainwright's evocative metaphor, the five women together "open a small fissure in the symbolic universe that the patrilineage constructs. Into this fissure can be drawn the memory of all the mothers and daughters who were likewise ancestors of Jesus."

It is a matter of interest that the four named female ancestors are not the revered Israelite matriarchs from Genesis, who would include Sarah, perhaps Hagar, Rebekah, Leah, and Rachel. Instead the text names Tamar, Rahab, Ruth, and the wife of Uriah. These women all found themselves at some point outside the patriarchal family structure, and consequently in danger. Their stories show how in the midst of their precarious situations they took unconventional initiatives to improve their lot. Furthermore, their enterprise becomes the vehicle for advancing the divine plan of redemption. In these instances, as Phyllis Trible says, "the brave and bold decisions of women embody and bring to pass the blessings of God." In the genealogy these four women foreshadow the mother of the Messiah, who found herself in a similarly perilous situation. She belongs in the company of these unconventional foremothers.

"Judah [was] the father of Perez and Zerah by Tamar." A childless widow, Tamar poses as a prostitute by the side of the road to seduce her father-in-law, Judah, who had reneged on his responsibility under the law of levirate marriage to continue his son's line. Her resulting illegitimate pregnancy brings the terrible sentence of death by burning. This is overturned only when Judah finds out about her ruse. Realizing that she had risked her life to continue the family line, he declares, "She is more righteous than I" (Gen. 38:26). She lives and brings forth twins. This is a powerful story of a woman's initiative and loyalty in the face of grave personal danger. As Jane Schaberg interprets the point, "Tamar herself has acted to secure her rights and demonstrate her righteousness. Suspected of bringing death and disgrace, she has in the end brought life," life in the form of the continuation of Judah's name and of the covenant promise of descendants for Abraham.

"Salmon [was] the father of Boaz by Rahab." A prostitute in Jericho, Rahab shelters the Israelite spies as they reconnoiter the city on their way back to the promised land. They had most likely sought her out initially in her professional capacity. In return for her hospitality and assistance in their escape, she secures a promise of safety for herself and her whole household when the Israelites finally attack. Basically "a survivor in the world of men at war," this Canaanite woman, though unfaithful to her own people, uses her ingenuity to ensure life for her loved ones along with success for Israel. Motivated by a measure of faith in Israel's God, she enters the list as a foremother in the blessed lineage of the Messiah. Even the New Testament holds her up as a model of faith and good works (Heb. 11:31; Jas. 2:25).

"Boaz [was] the father of Obed by Ruth." This young Moabite woman, widowed, childless, and poor, joins her aged mother-in-law Naomi in the struggle for survival in the patriarchal environs of Bethlehem. She secures a wealthy husband after crawling under his blanket and spending the night with him on the threshing floor, a story that has overtones of trickery and levirate obligation. It also carries a taint of scandal analogous to that of Tamar, who is, tellingly, mentioned by name in the people's blessing after Ruth gives birth to a son (Ruth 4:12). Though there is no clear evidence of seduction, Ruth risks an accusation of harlotry and is praised for taking that risk. She reverses her fortune, restores life to Naomi's line, and brings another measure of Gentile blood into the heritage of the Messiah.

"David was the father of Solomon by the wife of Uriah." This beautiful woman was the object of David's lust. Procuring her for himself, he commits adultery and has her husband killed on the front lines in war. The widow of a murdered man, she becomes pregnant with her lover's child. As punishment for David, this baby dies. Unlike the previous three women, Bathsheba does not at first exercise initiative but seems trapped in this appalling story, where her motives, feelings, rights, and love count for nothing before the power of the king. Her passivity changes, though, when she bears her next child, Solomon. Then as queen she acts to secure the throne for him from a dying David over the rights of an older brother, thereby also ensuring her own status for the rest of her life. As Schaberg points out, this foremother shows that God's providence goes forward overall in what happens in history, if not in every detail of the sordid, heartbreaking story.

Scholars have long sought a common point among these four ancestral women that would link them with the fifth woman named in Matthew's genealogy. One theory, first proposed by Jerome in the fourth century, holds that they were all sinners, in contrast to Mary. This, however, does not seem to be Matthew's point, because in the Jewish piety of the first century these women were looked upon with respect and praised for their deeds. Another hypothesis, popularized by Luther, proposes that they were all Gentiles, thereby indicating the scope of Jesus' redemptive mission beyond the Jewish people. But this is not necessarily the case for Tamar or Bathsheba, nor does it provide a point of similarity with Mary. A number of contemporary thinkers argue that the link among the women consists in the fact that (a) there is something extraordinary, irregular, even scandalous in their sexual activity, (b) which places them in some peril, (c) in view of which they take initiative, (d) thereby becoming participants in the divine work of redemption. Unexpectedly, God works through, with, and in them in a providential way to bring forth the Messiah. Pointing out that "in post-biblical Jewish piety these extraordinary unions and initiatives were seen as the work of the Holy Spirit," Raymond Brown argues that the genealogy presents these women and their actions as vehicles of divine providence, examples of how God moves in and through the obstacle of human scandal to bring about the coming of the Messiah. "Tamar was the instrument of God's grace by getting Judah to propagate the messianic line; it was through Rahab's courage that Israel entered the Promised Land; it was through Ruth's initiative that she and Boaz became the great-grandparents of King David; and it was through Bathsheba's intervention that the Davidic throne passed to Solomon." Through these unions, in which the woman was often the heroic figure, God carried forward the divine promise and plan. In straitened conditions the foremothers each dreamed of a future and acted to bring it about, thereby partnering God's redemptive work in history. Reading from a critical feminist perspective, Elaine Wainwright underscores the significance of the point that at the outset, none of these women is properly related to a man as wife or daughter. The fact that these foremothers, whether widowed, unmarried, prostitute, or separated from a spouse, exist independently outside traditional domestic arrangements makes them "dangerous to the patriarchal system." As they act, their stories encode aspects of women's power. And "God's messianic plan unfolds in and through such power." Jesus is as much the son of Tamar, Rahab, Ruth, and Bathsheba as he is of Abraham and David.

The presence of these anomalous women in Jesus' ancestry within the history of Israel frames the unconventional image of Mary as Matthew will describe her. In the genealogy she too exists outside the patriarchal family structure as the startling rupture of the patrilineage declares, "Jacob [was] the father of Joseph, the husband of Mary, of whom Jesus was born, who is called the Messiah" (1:16). Something odd is signified here. It is not Joseph who begets but Mary who gives birth. The patriarchal pattern is shattered, but as the foremothers show, "outside" this norm is not an easy place to dwell. Mary became pregnant without having had sex with Joseph, to whom she was betrothed in a legally binding relationship. In the eyes of society her pregnancy is a scandal damaging to the social order since she had not yet lived with her husband. She is vulnerable to the sanctions of the law and liable to receive rigorous punishment. Providentially, her story, like those of the women before her in the genealogy, has an outcome that ensures the birth of a child to carry on the covenant promise. In terms of giving us a picture of Mary's initiative or creative action in the midst of great danger, Matthew disappoints. She is voiceless in his narrative, which focuses on Joseph. Nevertheless, in her precarious predicament, she, along with her predecessors, "becomes the arena of sacred history and the locus where the divine promises to Israel" are carried forward and fulfilled.

It is precisely here, in the image of Mary as a scandalous woman with whom God identifies, that Jane Schaberg finds a powerful biblical theology. In a word, God acts as "one who sides with the outcast, endangered woman and child." Throughout the rest of Matthew's gospel, a stream of characters, from the hemorrhaging woman and crowds of other sick and disabled people to the Canaanite woman agitating for her little daughter's health, from the demoniac of Gadarene to the tax collector Matthew and his socially repugnant friends, will amplify this message first embodied in the genealogy's foremothers and in the mother of the Messiah. Insignificant, illegitimate, defenseless, tabooed people are beloved of God and may become agents of divine action in history. Jesus himself is the most radical instance of this divine compassion. Born of a non-Davidic woman yet messianic king, crucified by the state yet risen and ever present in the Spirit, Jesus illuminates in his life the presence of grace in people and situations branded sinful and shameful. "In a world racked with injustice," observes Donald Senior, "where the lament of promises never fulfilled and the frustration of hopes doomed to despair are the bitter bread of millions, the unconventional dimensions of the gospel portrayals of Mary seem to have more substance and appeal than ever before." Outside patriarchal expectations, looked upon askance by others, in danger for her life, her participation in the birth of Jesus is acclaimed as holy. Her female power is subversively linked to divine power and presence. In company with the four unorthodox women who act in the genealogy, she stands in solidarity with others in tragic or impoverished situations. Her memory bears the revolutionary gospel assurance that the God of Israel, the God revealed in Jesus, God's own Spirit, is with them.

Scandal and the Spirit

Matthew 1:18–25

THE WHIFF OF SCANDAL surrounding Mary in the genealogy becomes full-blown in the next episode, which recounts how she and her husband negotiate her unexpected pregnancy. Although the story is focused on Joseph and says nothing about Mary's action or faith, the "kernel" within the narrative is the female situation of Mary's conception of Jesus through the Spirit without reference to male begetting and the birth of the Messiah in these anomalous circumstances.

Recall that according to Jewish marriage customs of the day Mary and Joseph were bound together in a legally ratified marriage. The text is replete with references to "his wife," "your wife," and "your husband." Before they came to live together, Mary was found to be with child. Joseph knew he could not be the father. Her pregnancy would seem to be the result of adulterous behavior. Being a just man, upright and observant of Torah, he faced a searing dilemma. According to the Law, if a young betrothed woman is found, on first coming to her husband, to have previously lost her virginity, she shall be stoned to death. In the words of Deuteronomy, "they shall bring the young woman out to the entrance of her father's house and the men of her town shall stone her to death because she committed a disgraceful act. . . . So you shall purge the evil from your midst" (Deut. 22:20–27, at 21).

The one exception is if a young woman is raped in the open country as opposed to the city, for out there no one could hear her cries for help. Although this dictate was not carried out assiduously in first-century Palestine, its religious judgment on the nonvirginal bride would still wield power over an upright man. Mercifully, Joseph decided to divorce his wife quietly, thus sparing her any exposure to public shame, or worse. Just when the couple was on the verge of breaking up, an angel of the Lord appeared to Joseph in a dream encouraging him not to be afraid to take his wife to his home for "the child conceived within her is of the Holy Spirit." Here Matthew inserts a formulaic citation to show that this conception fulfills Isaiah's prophecy: "the virgin shall conceive and bear a son, and they shall call him Emmanuel" (Isa. 7:14). Faithful to his revelatory dream, Joseph completed the home-taking of the pregnant Mary: "he took her as his wife, but had no marital relations with her until she had borne a son; and he named him Jesus." By exercising the father's right to name the child, he acknowledged his wife's son as his own in the legal and public sense. The child born within this marriage will be regarded as his.

This narrative spells out the odd circumstances of Jesus' begetting hinted at in the genealogy. Like the four unconventional foremothers, Mary's situation is irregular. Her pregnancy is suspicious; socially and legally within patriarchal culture there is more than a hint of disrepute. Yet in the midst of this dangerous trouble something holy is going forward. God's Spirit moves amidst the threatening situation to bring about the birth of the Messiah. Both elements together, scandal and the Spirit, produce a tessera colored by the dialectic so characteristic of the gospel whose consummate event is the resurrection of the crucified one.

Historicity

Biblical scholars of all stripes think with more or less assurance that Matthew inherited an older, pre-gospel tradition that something was irregular about Mary's pregnancy. As Raymond Brown delicately puts it, people remembered that Jesus was born too early after his parents started to live together. There is a reasonable likelihood that this was the case, for why would the evangelist invent an embarrassment that he would then have to explain away? While the evangelist emphasizes that despite the scandal this child is the fruit of the action of the Holy Spirit, from earliest times readers have also wondered what the nature of the scandal actually was. Searching for the historical nucleus of the tradition of this too-early birth, present also in Luke's infancy narrative, thinkers from the second century onward have endorsed four different options. First, Joseph was the biological father who conceived Jesus with Mary while they were in the betrothal stage of their marriage. Second, an unknown man seduced Mary and committed adultery with her. Third, a Roman soldier, usually given the name Panthera, forcibly violated Mary, rape not being an unknown behavior in the Roman army. Fourth, it was a physical, biological miracle, the Holy Spirit of God causing the genesis of the child in Mary's womb in the absence of any human biological father. This last position, technically known as the virginal conception of Jesus, became and remains the official teaching of the Catholic Church, giving rise to the ancient appellation of Mary as Virgin Mother.

Contemporary scholarly discussion that attempts to assess the historical validity of each of these options gives them unequal weight. The Joseph-was-the-father thesis was first held by the Ebionites, an early group of mainly Jewish Christians who held that Jesus was not the Son of God from the beginning. Rather, he started his life simply as the son of Joseph, but in the course of time God adopted him as his own Son. This position has little backing in oral or written evidence. Indeed, Matthew's description of Joseph's quandary would seem to omit it out of court. By contrast, the charge of Jesus' illegitimacy by adultery or rape is clearly documented from the second century in both Jewish and Christian sources. It became a mainstay of anti-Christian polemic for centuries and also appears in Christian rebuttals. So well established did the paternity of the Roman soldier become in Jewish circles that simply the reference Ben Panthera, or son of Panthera, was sufficient to designate Jesus without mention of his given name. Raymond Brown and other exegetes argue that there is no way of knowing whether this charge arose before Matthew wrote, so that he was responding to it with the affirmation that Jesus was conceived by the Spirit, or whether in fact it originated as a derogatory interpretation of Matthew's gospel itself.

In an intensely thoughtful, respectful study of this charge, Jane Schaberg proposes that both Matthew and Luke inherited the tradition that Jesus the Messiah had been conceived in an illegitimate manner outside of marriage, along with the theological understanding that the Holy Spirit was in some way present and active in this event. "Both evangelists worked further with this potentially damaging and potentially liberating material," spinning it so artfully and with such theological astuteness that Christians soon became unaware of the illegitimacy that lay behind their infancy narratives. Trying to discern the contours of Mary's original trouble, Schaberg reads Matthew's text as a story "of a dangerous pregnancy outside the structures of patriarchal marriage—a situation as ancient as it is common," with chilling results on women's well-being throughout history. This reading draws the infancy narratives into the shadow of the cross, the larger scandal of the gospel. The good news, as already explored in the genealogy, is that God sides with the outcast, endangered woman and her child. God does this *not* by intervening directly to stop events of human violence and betrayal, to stop rape or conception after rape, but by being present "as one who reaches into that history to name the messiah." Through the creative power of the Spirit it comes about that "this child's existence is not an unpremeditated accident, and it is not cursed; the pregnant Mary is not to be punished." Rather, conceived of the Holy Spirit, this child has a special relation with God. Jesus is the Son of God, come to save his people from their sins. More profoundly than human beings could ever bring about by themselves, this disgrace turns out to be grace.

Schaberg admits that a major objection to her interpretation lies in the fact that we cannot prove that any early Christians read the infancy narratives as affirming an illegitimate conception. Arguing from a historical perspective, Amy-Jill Levine reasons that since Jewish charges of Jesus' illegitimate birth come from a time later than the composition of the gospel, it is unlikely that Matthew was interested in combating them in his opening chapter. While commending Schaberg's exegesis for challenging readers to pay attention to the perspective of women's experience, Barbara Reid demurs, "There is no doubt that her interpretation is possible, but the question remains whether the texts demand such an interpretation"; she is doubtful whether they do. In a similar vein Luise Schottroff, while respecting the healing power for violated women released by this exegesis, writes that "*measured against the texts*, I find that Schaberg's thesis fails to fit. As the text indicates, it was Joseph's mistaken belief that Mary had been seduced or sexually assaulted. Divine revelation corrects this false assumption," leaving us with a story that carries a profound critique of patriarchal dominance and violence. In my view, there is valuable insight in Schaberg's exegesis even if we grant that the critics are correct. She limns so clearly the consequences for a woman of that culture getting pregnant outside patriarchal social norms that even with belief in the virginal conception we begin to see the dangerous dilemma in which Mary was trapped according to Matthew's telling. Until Joseph's dream and his generous response, nothing but public disgrace, endless shame, perhaps a life of begging, perhaps even death loomed before her. The terror of her situation should be allowed once again to fertilize the Christian imagination, which has tended to "wrap Mary in an aura of romantic joy" at finding herself pregnant.

Contemporary persons have vastly differing reactions to this ancient charge of illegitimacy. Brown notes disapprovingly that some sophisticated Christian believers appreciate it as an example of the depths to which Christ descended when he "emptied himself" in becoming human. As an illegitimate son, Jesus would be counted among the outcasts for sure. It is not only worldly-wise Christians, however, who may find something religiously valuable in this interpretation, but women who are victims of sexual assault and all those in solidarity with them. Violence against women is a chief tool in the maintenance of patriarchy, one of whose defining tenets is man's right to woman's body. In traditional societies this right has been codified in law and custom to the extent of allowing honor killings of women pregnant outside of marriage. In contemporary democratic societies the struggle for women's right to the integrity of their own bodies, for the right to say no and be taken seriously, challenges patriarchal privilege at its core. In both situations, physical and psychological violence serves the cause of male domination and the litany of abuse is long and terrible, from witch burning to forcible rape (stranger rape, acquaintance rape, date rape, rape in marriage), from lesbian bashing to sadomasochistic pornography, from domestic abuse to serial murder, and yes, to slitting the throat of a young Tuareg girl found to be pregnant while betrothed. That the Spirit of God would be with a woman who suffered such violence, able to bring good from an inestimably painful situation, embodies the gospel in miniature and is a deep source of hope.

Devout persons unaware of early Christian history, on the other hand, may well find the charge that Jesus was conceived by seduction or rape utterly shocking. Dom Sebastian Moore recounts his own "devastating" experience when he first realized this theory had merit. "I lay awake all night, not even dozing, while a voice in my head kept saying over and over again, 'She's nothing but a whore, and the Church has made her into a Madonna, it's all a huge fake!' I felt my faith draining away." His crisis was resolved only when at a deep level he began to realize that to God "our petty social categories are nothing"; that while we have prettified the story of Jesus' conception, reducing it to something of a fairy tale, its reality points to a woman's faith, terrifying in its totality, in the mystery of God, who speaks from vast silence saying, "My ways are not your ways." We cannot begin to deal with the question of whether the virginal conception of Jesus is to be taken literally, he concludes, until we have recovered its spiritual significance from the travesty which the sexual immaturity of the Christian tradition has made of it, namely, a mother–son pattern from which the phallus is banished. This in turn has "powerfully reinforced the split image of Christian man, sexually dominating and spiritually sexless, and of Christian woman as virgin and mother but never as spouse." While insisting emphatically that a woman who has been raped is not a whore, I find Moore's analysis of the debilitating anti-sexual ethic that this story of Jesus' conception has buttressed to be astute. It runs on a parallel track to feminist existential if not political critique.

What then of the fourth position, the virginal conception? Critical biblical methods make it difficult simply to assume that miraculous conception by the Holy Spirit is historically the case, though they certainly do not rule it out either. To begin with, there is the troubling fact that there is no explicit reference to the virginal conception outside of the infancy narratives of Matthew and Luke. The astounding silence of the rest of the New Testament, including Paul, Mark, and John, indicates that this belief was not known, or if known, was not considered an important part of Christian kerygma in the early decades of the church. In addition, the infancy narratives themselves are brilliant literary creations embellished with folkloric elements such as astrology, dreams, and visionary messages and enriched with creative adaptations of material from the Hebrew scriptures; their very genre precludes relying on them as accurate renderings of history. The fact that the infancy narratives are replete with post-resurrection titles for Christ indicates, furthermore, that they were composed more with theological intent than with desire for historical facticity in the sense that dominates modern discussion. Then too, in Galatians, Isaac is said to be "born according to the Spirit" without implications for his mother's virginity (Gal. 4:29). As a result of translation issues, furthermore, biblical scholars eschew an appeal to the prophecy of Isaiah to settle the issue of historicity. In its own time Isaiah's text did not point to a messiah but gave the sign of an imminent birth of a child who would illustrate God's providential care for people under threat. In the original Hebrew, the ʿalmâ who will conceive refers to a young woman of marriageable age, perhaps the current queen. The word itself does not primarily signify virginity, a point reinforced elsewhere, for example, in the Song of Solomon, where it refers to young women in the king's harem (Song 6:8; also Prov. 30:19). In the Greek translation of the Hebrew Bible, the Septuagint, ʿalmâ is rendered as *parthenos*, a word that normally does mean biological virgin. Even here, however, the word is not clinically precise, being used twice of Dinah after Shechem has raped her (Gen. 34:3). Most tellingly, the grammatical structure of Isaiah's prophecy points to a virgin who *will conceive*. The future tense implies that the girl now a *parthenos* will get pregnant, presumably in the normal way. Matthew's use of Isaiah's text to explain Jesus' being conceived of the Holy Spirit gives this ancient prophecy an utterly new interpretation in light of his own theology.

To raise the question of the nucleus of Matthew's conception story is to discover that there is no absolutely satisfactory answer on historical grounds alone. Most scholars agree that this evangelist intends to declare the virginal conception in a biological sense, ruling out any human father. Many also hold that this is the tradition he received. But as to what lies behind that tradition at the first stage of gospel formation, contemporary scholarly approaches to the gospels simply cannot settle the issue. Raymond Brown, who argues that both Matthew and Luke think Jesus was conceived without a human father, points out that they were just not interested in the historical facticity of this question with the intensity of our post-Enlightenment minds. In an early essay on the virginal conception, he concluded that "the totality of the *scientifically controllable* evidence," the kind of evidence that stems from eyewitnesses and flows through a traceable tradition without contradiction with other reliable tradition, "leaves an unresolved problem." At the end of his mammoth work *The*

Birth of the Messiah, he reiterates this position: "the resurvey of the evidence necessitated by this commentary leaves me even more convinced of that," namely, that the core evidence in the New Testament about how Mary conceived is inconclusive at a historical level. Similarly, the ecumenical scholars of *Mary in the New Testament* summarize: "we see no way in which a modern scientific approach to the gospels can establish the historicity of the virginal conception (or, for that matter, disprove it)." Consequently, acceptance of the historicity of the virginal conception rests on other grounds, most notably, belief in biblical inerrancy for Protestants or in the teaching of the church for Catholics, both of which authorities squarely maintain the biologically miraculous nature of Jesus' conception.

In reaching their conclusions about the unprovability of the virginal conception, biblical scholars are wise enough to point out that the assent of faith cannot be equated with affirmations of history. The morality of historical knowledge requires that if one asks a question about a historical event, the answer must be arrived at and verified by the canons of the discipline of history itself. The intellectual responsibility of the investigator into history, as into science, lies in respecting this ethic, in all honesty. Faith has to do with a different kind of knowledge, an awareness of God's gracious, saving intent and action in the world, along with trust that this is the ultimate meaning of the universe and of our lives. Biblical proclamation of this belief is carried in the ideas of ancient cultures from which our own culture departs in many instances. Addressing the question of scientific and historical discrepancies in the biblical text, Vatican II taught a clarifying principle. Faith requires that we believe not every literal detail, but what God wanted placed in the scriptures "for the sake of our salvation." Thus, the account in Genesis of creation in six days does not have to be interpreted as historically factual. So long as we believe that God alone ultimately created the world and everything in it, evolutionary theory can explain the origin of species without threatening faith. So too with the gospels. Their point is not to teach scientifically controlled history but to proclaim the good news of salvation coming from God through Jesus in the power of the Spirit and to evoke our life-defining response. In composing his birth narrative Matthew had this purpose clearly in mind. Despite the ambiguity of its history, the theological significance of this narrative of socially irregular pregnancy is the heart of the matter.

Theology

Placed at the opening of Matthew's gospel, the story of Jesus' irregular conception has as its purpose to inform the reader that Jesus is the Son of God. This the evangelist does by employing a motif that recurs throughout the New Testament, namely, that Jesus' divine sonship is revealed through the action of the Spirit. These two go together like fife and drum in a marching band: through the Spirit, Jesus is the Son of God. This belief arose in connection with the resurrection and then was read progressively back into the Messiah's life. The "backwards development" of this christological trajectory can be traced in specific texts. Paul first played this tune in view of the resurrection: Christ "was descended from David according to the flesh and was declared to be Son of God with power according to the Spirit of holiness by resurrection from the dead" (Rom. 1:3–4). Mark next sounded the tune at Jesus' baptism, where the Spirit descends like a dove while a voice from heaven declares, "You are my Son, my beloved; with you I am well pleased" (Mark 1:11). By the latter part of the first century when Matthew and Luke wrote, Christians were affirming that Jesus was the Son of God not only since his resurrection, and not only since his baptism, but from the very beginning of his human life. Both evangelists present this belief through the same music of the Spirit as the divine agent of Jesus' conception. The idea that Jesus was conceived of the Holy Spirit thus pushes affirmation of his divine sonship, already expanded from resurrection to ministry, back to conception and birth. John will extend Jesus' divine sonship back even further, to before his earthly conception, declaring, "In the beginning was the Word . . ." (John 1:1). It will take until the Council of Nicaea in 325 before a clear decision is made about how far back this "beginning" goes, namely, to all eternity.

Begetting through the Holy Spirit, then, is first of all a theological way of describing divine sonship. Jesus is from God. This being the key to the text, scholars are virtually unanimous in ruling out any interpretation that would have the Spirit acting as a male sexual partner to Mary. In the scriptures the Spirit is the agency of God's creative power and presence. Unlike what happens in Hellenistic myths, the Spirit does not function as a male partner in a sacred marriage between a deity and a woman. Indeed in this Matthean story, while the author gives no indication of how the conception actually took place, there is no hint of divine intercourse of any sort and no language that would suggest the birth of a hero after a male god impregnates a human woman. As Brown writes, "there is never a suggestion in Matthew or in Luke that the Holy Spirit is the male element in a union with Mary, supplying the husband's role in begetting. Not only is the Holy Spirit not male (grammatically feminine in Hebrew; neuter in Greek), but also the manner of begetting is implicitly creative rather than sexual." This intuition is borne out in

Christian vocabulary, which does not call the Spirit the father of Jesus. Despite a scenario all too frequently entertained by the literal imagination, it is simply not the case that God the Father or his Spirit inseminates Mary. Conception by the Spirit signifies rather that God is the creative origin of Jesus' being. This nonsexual theological interpretation of creation by the Spirit is strengthened when we employ the female symbolism of the Spirit in Jewish, Syrian, and Christian traditions. *Rûaḥ*, the vivifying power in the universe, "the great virginal, life-engendering mother of all the living," becomes in this instance the "divine mother of Christ" in collaboration with the endangered woman from Galilee. Spirit-Sophia and Mary together bring in the Christ.

In this light, Mary's being with child of, from, or through (*ek* in Greek) the Holy Spirit affirms Jesus' christological identity in analogy with the resurrection and baptism stories. These, in turn, draw their power from the creation stories in Genesis, redolent with the same pneumatological power. Just as the Spirit of God moved over the chaotic waters and danced a whole world into being, the same creative Spirit moved over the dead Jesus, the unknown Jesus at the start of his ministry, and the womb of Mary to create a new world. Gerhard Delling explains, "As the Spirit of God hovered over formless matter when the miracle of creation took place, so there is a new creative act of God when Jesus is born." In addition to revealing the identity of Jesus as Son of God, the theological significance of Jesus' being conceived by the Holy Spirit now becomes profound. This story signals that God freely takes the initiative in the advent of the Messiah. The Savior's coming depends not in the first place on human decisions but on God's own incalculable desire to be among suffering, sinful human beings in the flesh. Ontologically Jesus' origin lies in God the Most High. His existence has its foundation in God. He is born wholly of grace, wholly of promise, God's gracious gift to humankind. The *novum* of his approach lies in the incomprehensible depths of the mercy of God. That this requires the human cooperation in different ways of a poor Galilean couple at first vastly troubled by the gift does not diminish the power of divine initiative that blesses the world with a new act of creation by the Creator Spirit.

This line of reasoning leads a number of theologians to conclude that neither the New Testament nor magisterium of the church fundamentally teaches that the virginal conception is first of all a miracle of nature. To do that, you would have to argue that Matthew and Luke had this one essential purpose in mind when they were writing their infancy narratives, which they clearly did not. Frans Jozef von Beeck makes the fine distinction that "calling the virginal conception and birth a miracle is a conclusion from the data of faith, not an article of faith in and of itself." Given the commonly available understanding of the physiological processes leading to conception in their day, whereby the mother supplied the physical mass, the father supplied the vital spirit that ignites it to form an embryo, and God supplied the soul, the evangelists told their infancy stories as "missionary theophanies." Using the cultural assumptions of the day, they intended to say that Jesus was a child of his mother, and hence fully human, while affirming that God's own holy will is the sole true initiator of this child who is the world's Savior: "in loving mercy, God and God alone takes the initiative in having the divine Power and Wisdom dwell among us as one of us."

Granted that in scripture and the creeds "conceived by the Holy Spirit" is not in the first instance a biological but an evocative theological statement, our minds, imbued with contemporary scientific knowledge of how conception takes place, inevitably return to the historical issue and ask How? Where did the Y chromosome come from? With what sperm did Mary's egg unite to initiate a new human being? Theologically, the answer is that in a new act analogous to the creation of the world, the Creator Spirit created the Y chromosome *ex nihilo* and caused it to appear in Mary's body without sexual intercourse. As Brown reiterates, "It was an extraordinary action of God's creative power, as unique as the initial creation itself." Contemporary debate arises when some scholars query whether this is really necessary. Given the biblical witness to divine modes of acting whereby divine agency normally works in tandem with human agency—through secondary causes, in scholastic terminology—the Spirit of God can be seen to work in and through what happens in the world to lure it toward fulfillment. Divine and human fatherhood are not necessarily mutually exclusive. The action of God does not have to replace or cancel natural sexual activity so as to render the human role superfluous. Indeed, since sex is God's own good design for procreation, would it not be more suitable that God use it in this instance?

In thinking this through, it is important to note that the virginal conception is not necessary to account for the sinlessness of Jesus, which is present in other layers of New Testament tradition that know nothing of this belief. Later developments will link sex with sinfulness, but in the infancy narratives there is no trace of antisexual bias that would demean ordinary conception in marriage as less than holy. Later Christian teaching will use the virginal conception as imaginative shorthand for the doctrine of two natures, picturing that God the Father gave Christ a divine nature while Mary his mother gave him a human nature. But in orthodox Christian belief Jesus would be God's beloved child no matter how he was conceived because his sonship is eternal and independent of earthly incarnation. Joseph Ratzinger explains this clearly, beginning with the difference between birth stories of heroes in the history of religions and the birth story of Jesus in the gospels:

> The main contrast consists in the fact that in pagan texts the Godhead almost always appears as fertilizing, pro-creative power, thus under a more or less sexual aspect and hence in a physical sense as the "father" of the savior-child. As we have seen, nothing of this sort appears in the New Testament: the conception of Jesus is new creation, not begetting by God. God does not become the biological father of Jesus, and neither the New Testament nor the theology of the Church has fundamentally ever seen in this narrative or in the event recounted in it the ground for the real divinity of Jesus. . . . According to the faith of the Church the Sonship of Jesus does not rest on the fact that Jesus had no human father; the doctrine of Jesus' divinity would not be affected if Jesus had been the product of a normal human marriage. For the Sonship of which faith speaks is not a biological but an ontological fact, an event not in time but in God's eternity.

A begetting by divine power through the Holy Spirit always remains *analogous* to human begetting and needs to be understood by appreciating the myriad ways Spirit-Sophia works in the world. In this light, the gospel story of the conception of the Messiah by the Holy Spirit places Mary with the life-giving powers of her body at the heart of Sophia-God's approach to the world. Conceived by the Holy Spirit, the Messiah was born of the virgin Mary.

Scandal and the Spirit

The historical and theological issues of Matthew's conception story receive yet another reading in feminist interpretation. The text of Matthew's birth narrative is filled with tension. While on the surface this is a story shaped by patriarchal law, the narrative is encircled by female images, from the creative Spirit evoked by grammar and imagery to the endangered pregnant woman. It features Joseph as the recipient of divine revelation while at the same time honoring a woman's conception of a child outside of patriarchal norms. It underscores the disgrace that surrounds her condition but affirms emphatically that God stands with the endangered woman and her child to the point where they are the fulfillment of divine promise. Feminist insight into both the scandal and the power of the virgin woman fruitful with the Spirit uncovers unsuspected empowerment for women in this story and gives reason to honor the virginal conception in full strength.

This story of illicit pregnancy places Mary in solidarity with women who suffer violence or the threat of violence from patriarchal authority, affirming against all social consensus that God is with them. Even with the emphasis on Joseph's upright and good-hearted actions, Mary is in danger from her irregular pregnancy. When the story opens, she has no guarantee of her own safety. Then as now in patriarchal society, female virginity functions in a masculinist system of exchange which women violate at their own risk. The story resolves the problem by having her husband ultimately offer safety and legitimacy to his wife and the fetus growing within her, thus bringing them back into the male-dominated order upheld by society. At the same time, and here is the major twist, it demonstrates that patriarchal logic fails to do justice to God's ways. Mary is in jeopardy, but God stands with her to fulfill the ancient promise. Her child appears to be illegitimate but is called holy, the one who will save the people from their sins. Bearing the Messiah outside of patriarchal norms, Mary yet moves within the divine plan of salvation. While reverberating with a tone of scandal, the narrative thus subtly challenges the biased social patterns that create the scandal to begin with. In the end, Mary's validation shows that "the reproductive power of woman and her role in the birth of the Messiah are affirmed outside the patriarchal structure." Not only that, but being "outside" is precisely where the encounter with the Holy One takes place. "Mary is a woman who has access to the sacred outside the patriarchal family and its control"; in her precarious state she helps to birth the work of the Spirit. Matthew is no feminist, but it would be hard to write a story that more strongly honors the importance to God of a woman at severe risk for violating the expectations of patriarchal marriage. The shadow cast by her scandalous situation connects in hope with oppressed women struggling by the power of God's Spirit to survive patriarchal violence and the threat of violence. Elaine Wainwright proposes that because of the way it speaks to women's situation, this story itself was kept alive in house churches where there was a living praxis of women in leadership.

This tessera also plays into the current retrieval of the meaning of virginity as a symbol of female autonomy. As we have seen, the symbol of virginity does not necessarily refer in the first instance to the absence of sexual experience. Historians of religion have discovered a raft of virgin goddesses who take lovers but are still considered to be virgins in the sense that they are free from male control, not accessories to men or dependent on their protection. To be virgin is to be one-in-yourself, free, independent, unsubordinated, unexploited, a woman never subdued. In this sense, the virginal conception is valuable in bearing a message of revolutionary female empowerment. The virgin Mary's conception of the Messiah without male begetting epitomizes in its own strange way women's strong abilities in collaboration with divine Spirit. The male is excluded. The end of the patriarchal order is announced. In her often quoted "Ain't I a Woman?" speech, Sojourner Truth voices this insight with unsurpassed eloquence. I quote here from the account published in the "National Anti-Slavery Standard" in 1863. After insisting on her own humanity as a woman in the face of dehumanizing experiences of slavery and male prejudice, she continues:

> "That little man in black there, he say a woman can't have as much rights as a man, 'cause Christ wasn't a woman. Where did your Christ come from?" Rolling thunder could not have stilled that crowd as did those deep, wonderful tones, as she stood there with out-stretched arms and eyes of fire. Raising her voice still louder, she repeated, "Where did your Christ come from? From God and a woman! Man had nothing to do with him!" Oh, what a rebuke she gave the little man.

This emancipated slave, abolitionist, and independent preacher, illiterate but steeped in wisdom, recognized anti-woman nonsense being spouted by a clergyman and stood up to set the record straight. God and a woman together brought the Messiah into the world. They did so in partnership, divine *rûaḥ* and a woman of low social status collaborating together, without the intervention of men. All the placid, sentimental paintings of madonna and child cannot rob this gospel story of its raw, subversive implications. It supports the integrity of women's spiritual power when they listen to the blowing of the Spirit in their lives. It affirms their abilities

to create new, saving possibilities outside of patriarchal structures and in the teeth of reactionary violence. The account of
Mary's being with child from the Holy Spirit adds the color of
danger to the marian mosaic, tinted with a striking hue of
female power in partnership with God.

Wisdom from the East

Matthew 2:1–12

WHEN JESUS WAS BORN in Bethlehem a group of magi, number unknown, followed a star from the East to pay homage to this newborn king of the Jews. Their route took them through the capital city Jerusalem, where their encounter with Herod the Great, Rome's client-king of the Jews, filled the palace coterie with alarm. Pushing on, "they rejoiced exceedingly with great joy" when they saw the star stop. "Going into the house they saw the child with Mary his mother, and they knelt down and paid him homage," offering gifts of gold, frankincense, and myrrh. Warned in a dream not to let Herod know where the child was, they went home by another route.

The Christian imagination has long conflated the infancy narratives of Matthew and Luke, but the two are very different at this point. Luke's story begins in the northern village of Nazareth and uses a Roman-ordered census to move Mary and Joseph south to Bethlehem, David's ancestral home and therefore the birthplace of the Messiah. Matthew works in reverse. His account begins in Bethlehem, then brings the family up to Nazareth by a circuitous route laid down by his theological interest, moving them into and out of Egypt. Matthew knows nothing of a census or of birth in a stable, of being laid in a manger, of shepherds keeping watch over their flocks and angels singing. Instead, this family already dwells in Bethlehem, seemingly as long-term inhabitants. A sign that they are settled rather than transient is that they live in a house, a secure residence, which the magi enter when they reach the goal of their quest. There is no scholarly agreement over which account, Luke's or Matthew's, is more factual, if either, but that is not the point. Their intent is to inform us, as their gospels open, of the christological identity of this child, and they go about it in different ways. Three elements color this tessera of the marian mosaic.

The presence of danger from patriarchal law that ran through the story of Mary's conception grows stronger here with the introduction of Herod, who embodies the menace of the state. Recall his tenure as Rome's point-man in Palestine, to whom the interests of his own people mattered little. His ostentatious living, opulent building projects, excessive taxation, and extravagant cruelty laid a more than heavy burden on the peasant population. Would such a tyrant care to hear that there is a contender for his throne? Indeed, the messianic title King of the Jews appears here in its sole appearance outside the passion narrative, where it was nailed to the cross of Jesus. Suffering looms on the horizon.

The presence of wisdom is signaled by the arrival of seekers from the East, knowledgeable about a wisdom tradition that has led them to search for the new liberator. Although pictured as kings in the popular imagination, they are technically magi, a term that referred historically to people engaged in the mystic, supernatural arts. These included astronomers, priestly augurers, fortune tellers, and magicians of varying plausibility. Whichever mode of discernment they used, magi in general carried out the religious function of trying to interpret the will of the gods. Wainwright offers the feminist suggestion that Matthew's magi may evoke the wisdom tradition of scripture with its many points of contact with foreign religion, including female images of God. They could be following the star of Sophia God, a suggestion made more cogent because Holy Wisdom is used to interpret Jesus in key places later in this gospel. In Brown's opinion, the magi represent the wise and learned among the Gentiles who come to believe in Christ. They epitomize "the best of pagan lore and religious perceptivity which has come to seek Jesus through revelation in nature," that is, through the star. On their journey their wisdom is enriched by the revelation in the Jewish scriptures uncovered by Herod's scribes, and completed by finding the Messiah himself. Like some of the foremothers of the genealogy, they signal that Jesus is destined for Gentiles as well as Jews. Taking a less literary, more political view, Richard Horsley notes that since magi served as priestly advisers to kings in the Roman-occupied eastern territories, they would stand in opposition to the tyranny of the empire. It was not only the Jewish people who resisted Roman rule. Hence their following the star and giving obeisance to a new and different kind of king expresses their hope for liberation from oppressive rule. Jesus is attended by wise ones whose wisdom makes them figures of resistance; their tribute signals the attraction of the coming reign of God, which will bring about salvation as liberation. Whichever interpretation one chooses, the appearance of these exotic strangers is a mixed blessing. It is the first public acknowledgment of the messianic identity of Mary's child, but it brings in its wake a drumbeat of peril. The visit of the magi has drawn the unwelcome attention of the powerful to the existence of this young, vulnerable family.

The presence of the house in this episode signals an ideal for the church. The drama of good and evil being played out between the danger of Herod and the wisdom of the magi focuses on the house wherein is found "the child with Mary his mother." Recognized by her own name and her relation-

ship to the messianic child, Mary along with her husband
receives these seekers, their gifts, and their wisdom from the
East. Allied with unconventional foremothers, surviving the
scandal of an irregular pregnancy, now nurturing a young
child, she is linked from the outset to the core of the new
thing God is doing in this world. Unfortunately, Matthew
gives her no words to say or actions to take. But we can read
her presence in this climactic revelatory scene as an "extraordinary inclusion" with subversive implications for women's
participation in the Jesus movement. After Jesus' death and
resurrection, the primary locale for this movement throughout the first century was the house church. Members of different social classes, races, and genders gathered in houses
across the Greco-Roman world to remember, ritually celebrate, and proclaim the good news of salvation in Christ and
to test its implications for the way they lived. In this context
Matthew employs the "house" as a continuous metaphor for
the church. What goes on in the house in various passages of
his gospel evokes the ideal for his community, at the center of
whose life lay the house church (Michael Crosby). The magi
with their gifts enter the Bethlehem house and find Christ. As
a result, relationships are realigned. In terms of class and
social status, "aristocrats acknowledge a child, and resources
are shared when the rich give to an ordinary Judean family,
one which probably represented the majority of Jewish families impoverished by Herodian, Roman, and temple taxation."
So too, implies Matthew, should economic resources to sustain life be shared in the house church. In terms of gender, the
magi find Mary in the house, named and at the center of the
scene. So too, implies the story, visited by the liberating wisdom of Christ, the church should realign old patriarchal patterns of relationship that marginalize women and move to

partnership in the following of Christ. Wainwright suggests that this message was heard in house churches where women took active roles, at least "in the Matthean households who did not take offense at such a challenge." Readers today can still hear this radical invitation.

Refugees from Slaughter

Matthew 2:13–23

THIS TESSERA PLACES Mary at the center of an experience of terror and displacement. Herod stalked the trail of the magi, a menacing reminder that "while the star of the newborn King has shone forth in purity and simplicity, there are those who will seek to blot out that light." In a towering rage Herod sought to kill his newborn rival. Warned in a dream, Joseph took "the child and his mother" and went fleeing by night into Egypt. Back in Bethlehem, soldiers butchered all the male children under two years of age. After Herod died, Joseph, guided by yet another dream, returned with "the child and his mother" to the land of Israel. Warned again in a dream that despotic Archelaus had inherited his father's rule in Judea, Joseph headed the family north to Galilee, where they made their home in the town of Nazareth. Riveting images impress themselves on the imagination: terrible fear propelling escape in the dark from oncoming murder with no guarantee of success; the iron swords, the baby blood, the red pavement stone, the empty look of mothers mute with shock, their piercing wails of inconsolable grief; a young family's life in exile in a foreign land, negotiating strange language, customs, and institutions, all the while carrying memories of horror and a feeling of pain for those who did not escape; the recognition that you can't go home again and the brave setting out in a new direction.

This story lifts up a memory of Mary with her husband and child in agonized solidarity with the millions of refugees struggling to survive in a harsh world even today. War is "pure hell on earth" for civilian victims, reads a letter from the U.N. High Commission for Refugees; those particularly at risk are children, late-term pregnant women, and the elderly. The twentieth century, continuing into the twenty-first, has witnessed "a staggering tide of uprooted people" stretching from Afghanistan to Sudan to Chechnya to Palestine to East Timor to Haiti, a flood of fleeing millions on five continents. Their basic survival is at stake as hunger, dehydration, and lack of shelter and medical care take their toll, along with the trauma of violence, separation from family members, and ongoing fear and anxiety. This is a crisis that does not last only a day but drags on in the chronic poverty of refugee camps and the blockading of hope for the future. "Over 2,000 years ago, Mary and Joseph sought shelter far from their homeland. Today, millions like them continue to search for a safe place to rest," writes the Catholic Relief Services newsletter. "There are few things more traumatic than losing your family's home." Even if home is a modest shack, it is where people come for refuge and rest, the place where they keep their possessions and cooking utensils, the place where they raise their children and keep the family safe. "Losing the home will put a family on a downward slide into deeper poverty and vulnerability." Millions of lives are uprooted this way because of political disaster. In a similar way, Joseph and Mary fled their house and their homeland with their baby for political reasons, to escape the murderous wrath of their country's ruler. Sri Lankan theologian Tissa Balasuriya makes the astute observation that once arrived in Egypt, Joseph would be akin to a migrant worker, a non-national willing to do even the most menial tasks in order to survive. "For many years, Mary along with Joseph would have experienced tribulations by being foreign workers in Egypt. In this, too, she experienced personally the problems which many of the underprivileged people even in rich countries have to face. . . . It is a pity that popular devotions to Mary do not recall her in this experience as a poor, courageous woman."

Later apocryphal gospels sought to make the flight into Egypt into a triumphal procession for the Son of God. Native African lions and leopards in a docile mood led the caravan through the desert: "wherever Joseph and holy Mary went, they went before them, showing them the way and lowering their heads in worship; they showed their servitude by wagging their tails, and honored Him with great reverence" (*Gospel of Pseudo-Matthew* 19.1). Palm trees bent down to refresh the weary pilgrims with fruit; springs of water appeared in the desert. Their arrival showed Egyptian religion with its 365 gods and goddesses to be false: "But it came to pass that when blessed Mary entered the temple with the child, all the idols fell to the ground, so that they all lay on their faces completely overturned and shattered. Thus they openly showed that they were nothing" (*Gospel of Pseudo-Matthew* 23). The respect of the native Egyptians, including their military commanders, followed. Would that every refugee had it so good. Matthew's original text gives no hint of such an easy escape but positions this young family on the road of exile and deprivation.

Even if not historically factual, the narrative of infant massacre and escape to Egypt reflects the historical situation that prevailed in Jewish Palestine under Roman and Herodian rule. Using death and destruction as a means of intimidating people, the imperial occupiers and their client-kings created thousands of refugees. When military action commenced, people were forced to flee from their homes if they wanted to avoid being killed. The text also accurately mirrors the character of Herod, who indulged in well-attested acts of ruthless cruelty. He had three of his own children put to death on various pretexts. To ensure proper mourning at his own funeral, he instructed his soldiers to kill notable political prisoners upon news of his death: "So shall all Judea and every household weep for me, whether they wish it or not." The brutality gene was passed on to his son Archelaus, who ushered in his reign with a massacre of three thousand people and was so despised for his dictatorial ways that he was finally deposed by Rome. Carnage, upheaval, loss of home and neighbors, children caught in a web of violence, parents in despair—this story was all too intelligible to readers in Matthew's time, and in our own.

By the way the evangelist shapes this sequence, artfully inserting fulfillment citations from the Hebrew scriptures, he inlays announcements about the christological identity of this child into this story of narrow escape from death. Jesus recapitulates the formative history of the people of whom he is the new, redemptive flowering. Recall how Israel went down to Egypt at the instigation of Jacob and there found refuge from famine. Recall the rescue of the infant Moses from the evil intent of Pharaoh to kill the male babies. Recall the liberating exodus of the enslaved Hebrew people from Egypt. "Out of Egypt I have called my son," the gospel quotes the prophet Hosea (Hos. 11:1), referring now to Jesus but harking back to the original exodus of the people who were God's beloved children. Jesus is the king of the Jews in a theological way that Herod never could be.

A second citation positions this family in relation to the violence. Recall how in the course of Israel's history first the northern and then the southern tribes were led away into exile, a state of banishment from which only a minority returned. "A voice was heard in Ramah, weeping and loud lamentation, Rachel weeping for her children; she refused to be consoled, because they are no more," the gospel quotes the prophet Jeremiah (Jer. 31:15), referring now to the Bethlehem mothers but evoking the captivity and deportation centuries earlier of the tribes descended from their ancient foremother. This infancy story thus deliberately echoes the two great paradigmatic events in Israel's history, exodus and exile, connecting the endangered Messiah with the history of the Jewish people. Tellingly, it affirms the manner in which God's salvific power operates, namely, in the midst of and not above the struggles of history. Emmanuel, his mother, and her dreamy, practical husband retrace the biblical pattern of exile and exodus and end up in Nazareth according to God's salvific design.

In an intense and unusual way, there are multiple references to "the child and his mother" throughout this episode. The repetition of this phrase in verses 13, 14, 20, and 21 establishes a powerful connection between mother and child in this situation of peril. Both are threatened. Mary has already faced down danger from patriarchal virginity laws, but now her life is once again at risk from the brutal power of the state. The vulnerable child being hunted is never alone but is always in the company of his mother, surrounded, the text implies, by her fierce care, which exposes her to the same peril. Jesus here is indeed "Miriam's child." Repeated allusions to her presence, furthermore, keep punctuating the story with a female center of interest which serves to decenter the exercise of male military and political power that governs this narrative. Her character once again opens a fissure in the symbolic universe of patriarchy. "The infant Jesus is located throughout in the presence of the woman Mary, designated in the text as 'his mother' but evocative of those women whose anomalous stories challenge patriarchal family structures." Connected with the genealogy, the continuously named presence of Mary in this scene evokes the power and presence of women in Israel's history and the birth of its Messiah. Empowering hearers of this gospel who struggle for women's full participation in the Christian mission, this interpretation allows those threatened by patriarchal violence to themselves constitute an internal counterthreat to the status quo.

Neither Mary nor the Bethlehem mothers speak aloud or otherwise react to the slaughter of the children. The voice of Rachel weeping resounds in this silence. Long a symbolic figure of the suffering mother, more specifically of the nation mourning its lost peoples, even more precisely of Jewish mothers, whose children were murdered on a mass scale, this ancestral figure enters the story to send up their lament to God. They bond together as she articulates their grief, allowing their outrage to cry to heaven. Her tears and loud lamentation rip still another fissure in this well-ordered text. "It is the raised voice of Rachel that pierces the male world of power, of slaughter, and of divine favor," rejecting even the divine plan that would rescue one special child but ignore the rest. Her tears gush forth as resistance to such brutality, her shouts as a challenge to this violent way of running the world. Subverting the patriarchal pattern, this "female image of the compassionate, inconsolable mother provides a counterpoint to the extreme violence of the holocaust of the male children at the hand of the male ruler, Herod." Since the later verses of this Rachel poem in Jeremiah depict divine compassion in female imagery as the love of a mother for the child of her womb, Rachel also points to the motherly God who weeps inconsolably in protest with those who are bereaved (Jer. 31:20).

One day the authority of the imperial state will get Mary's son too. His close, heart-in-the-mouth brush with death in infancy will turn all too real in his thirties, and his mother's lament will take a newly sharp, personal turn. The good news of the gospel is that the advent of God focused in Jesus, who is descended not only from Abraham and David but also from the defiantly lamenting Rachel and the threatened, fleeing, defiantly surviving Mary, compassionately overcomes the worst outrage. This is the Christian hope. But given the river of deaths of millions of children due to military and domestic assault and the institutional violence of poverty, "Rachel still weeps in every country of the world" (Megan McKenna). Borrowing phrases from Mary's Magnificat, one contemporary poet imagines her resonating with her grieving ancestor, saying:

> Wail, mourn aloud, sister Rachel . . .
> Unleash grief's force, sister Rachel, to change what
> made you grieve . . .
> Unleash grief's force, sister Rachel, the mighty to bring
> down, the wealthy to chase out, the hungry to fill
> up . . .
> Of your child you are deprived; let no one steal your
> rage.

Annunciation:
Call of the Prophet

Luke 1:26–38

As WE BEGIN to examine the tesserae painted by Luke, one color runs through them all. Mary is a disciple, not in the historical sense that she accompanied Jesus during his ministry, but in the existential sense that she heard the word of God and acted upon it. This view comes to the fore in an exchange unique to this gospel. Moved by Jesus' preaching, an admiring woman in the crowd raised her voice to cry, "Blessed is the womb that bore you and the breasts that you sucked!" This was a typical Mediterranean expression that praised a mother for the fine qualities of her son. In reply Jesus emphasized qualities of spirit, saying, "Blessed rather are those who hear the word of God and keep it!" (Luke 11:27–28). Some few interpreters think that with the word "rather" Jesus set up a contrast between true believers and his mother. This explanation does not hold up, however, in view of the positive way Luke presents Mary in all other scenes of his gospel. Instead, the intensifier "rather" means yes, what you said is true as far as it goes, but there is more to be said. In effect, Jesus' beatitude echoes that of Elizabeth, who early on had saluted the young woman pregnant with the Messiah with the words, "Blessed is she who believed . . ." (Luke 1:45). In Luke's theology the faith that marks a genuine disciple consists in hearing and acting upon God's word. The next five mosaic stones, taken from his work, present Mary as just such an exemplary disciple in ever varying scenarios.

The annunciation scene, which appears after the announcement of the birth of John the Baptist, depicts Mary with a mood of celebration as a hearer and doer of God's word. The angel Gabriel was sent from God to a young, unlettered woman in Nazareth, a poor village in the oppressed peasant region of Galilee. The girl is betrothed to a man named Joseph, but in accord with Jewish marriage customs has not yet moved into his house to share life together. The heavenly messenger announces God's desire that Mary bear a child who will be great, the Messiah, the holy Son of God. Assured that the Spirit will empower and protect her, she gives her free consent, casting her lot with the great work of redemption in the belief that nothing is impossible with God.

The overarching purpose of this story, as with Matthew's opening narrative, is to disclose to Luke's readers at the outset the truth about Jesus' messianic identity. Using christological titles and language developed by the church after the resurrection, the scene vividly dramatizes the theological point that Jesus did not just become the Son of God after his death (Paul) or even at his baptism (Mark) but is the Son of God from his very conception in this world. At the same time, by making Mary the central character, Luke's text invites reflection on her faith and action in her own right. Indeed, throughout centuries of translation and reflection, no other text has had more influence on the development of mariology, for better or worse. At its worst, the emphasis of some interpreters on the phrasing of Mary's response, "be it done to me according to your word," has led to that ideal of woman as an obedient handmaid, passively receptive to male commands, which women today find so obnoxious. But other interpretations are possible. By examining three facets of this text, namely, its literary structure, language about the Holy Spirit, and the import of Mary's consent, we can draw this rich scene into a liberating memory replete with "lessons of encouragement."

Literary Structure

In this scene Luke deftly combines two conventions of biblical narrative, the birth announcement and the commissioning of the prophet. Both types of stories follow the same literary structure, which in its complete form comprises five standard elements. First, an angel or some other form of messenger from heaven appears with a greeting. Next, the recipient reacts with fear or awe and is encouraged not to be afraid. Third, central to the story, the announcement itself declares God's intent and gives a glimpse of what the future outcome will be. Fourth, the recipient then offers an objection: How so? Fifth, the story ends with a sign of divine power that reassures the recipient. This story pattern is used at significant junctures in Israel's history both to announce the coming birth of a significant child and to describe the call of adult persons into collaboration with God's designs. The scriptures are replete with examples. A birth story: when the Israelites were groaning under a foreign oppressor, an angel of the Lord appeared to a barren woman, wife of Manoah, to declare that she would conceive and bear a son who would deliver Israel from the hand of the Philistines. The dynamism of the structured story line runs on, ending with the sign of the angel ascending in the flame of the sacrificial altar, followed by the birth of Samson, in whom the Spirit stirred at an early age (Judg. 13:2–23). In a similar fashion, the classic birth announcement heralds the coming of Ishmael to Hagar, Isaac to Abraham and Sarah, John the Baptist to Zechariah and Elizabeth, and Jesus to Joseph (in Matthew's gospel). The Christmas morning gospel presents a familiar example in the story of angels appearing to the shepherds, which follows the pattern of appearance, fear and reassurance, message about the birth of the Messiah, and the sign of a babe in swaddling clothes lying in a manger. By using this fixed literary pattern to announce the birth of Jesus to Mary, Luke is linking mother and child to the great sweep of God's gracious history with Israel and heralding the significance of this child in that history.

Luke fuses this function of the announcement story with the second scriptural use of this literary form, which is to call and commission a prophet. One particularly telling example is the story of Moses (Exod. 3:1–14). While he is shepherding flocks in the desert, (1) the angel of the Lord appears to him in a burning bush; (2) Moses takes off his shoes, hides his face in fear; (3) then comes the message: God has seen the misery of the people enslaved in Egypt, has heard their cries, feels what they are suffering, and has come down to deliver them: "Come I will send you to Pharaoh to bring my people, the Israelites, out of Egypt"; (4) Moses' objection follows as the night the day: "Who am I?" too slow of speech; (5) finally, God gives assurance with the indelible words "I will be with you," coupled with a sign in the form of a future promise that, once freed, the people will worship on this very mountain. Here the five-point pattern of the announcement story narrates the moment when Moses, prophet and liberator, enters into his life's vocation. It signals God's intent to deliver an enslaved people, for which task a human being is chosen and for which this person's free assent is essential. Once the die is cast, the presence of God will guide this person through thick and thin, and the community will remember him with gratitude for the ways in which his response brought blessing upon the oppressed people. In the beginning, though, it is a religious encounter that transpires in the solitude of the heart before God: the exiled shepherd, the flaming bush, the prophetic call, the free response, all embedded in the tradition of a community now struggling for freedom.

Another clear instance of this pattern at work is the story of Gideon, set in a time when the people were groaning under conquerors from the land of Midian (Judg. 6:11–24). The angel of the Lord appears under an oak tree; Gideon's fear is met with the classic reassurance, "The Lord is with you"; then comes the message that Gideon is to deliver Israel from the oppressive hand of Midian: "I hereby commission you"; but, objects Gideon, my clan is the weakest of all; nevertheless, "I will be with you," and the sign is fire that consumes his sacrificial bread and meat. The call of other prophets and liberators in the history of Israel often follows this pattern, Jeremiah being another memorable example.

Luke's artistry welds the announcement of Jesus' birth to the call of Mary as a woman commissioned by God. Biblical scholars point out that in this scene she is engaged for a prophetic task, one in a long line of God-sent deliverers positioned at significant junctures in Israel's history. All five elements of the literary convention march in full, vigorous display. The angel appears with the classic greeting "Hail, favored one, the Lord is with you," a formula often used to greet a person chosen by God for a special purpose in salvation history. Mary reacts with a troubled heart and receives the classic encouragement not to be afraid. The messenger announces that she will conceive a child who will be great, son of the Most High, inheriting the throne of David in a kingdom without end. Her objection "How can this be?" is met with the promise that the Holy Spirit will be with her. The promise is underscored with the sign of old Elizabeth's pregnancy. Replete with angelic voice, fear and reassurance, message, objection, and sign, this is a story of Mary being commissioned to carry forward God's design for redemption. The announcement of her impending motherhood is at the same time her prophetic calling to act for the deliverance of the people. She now takes her place "among those prophets called to give word and witness to the hidden plan of God's salvific activity not yet seen by other members of the community of faith." Her affirmative response to this divine initiative sets her life off on an adventure into the unknown future. The divine presence will be with her through good times and bad, and ultimately the community will remember her life with gratitude. In this scene the whole story is captured in its beginning: it is a prophetic vocation story of a Jewish girl and her God, set within the traditions of her people struggling for freedom.

Holy Spirit

At the center of this story lies a powerful declaration of the relationship between this peasant woman and the Spirit of God. In good standard fashion Mary has objected, "How can this be since I do not know man?" The angel replies, "The Holy Spirit will come upon you, and the power of the Most High will overshadow you," and thus the child will be called holy, Son of God. By the fourth and fifth centuries, once church councils had declared the doctrinal identity of Jesus Christ to be that of one person in two natures, human and divine, the Christian imagination interpreted this Lukan text in a literally sexual way. Mary the virgin was somehow impregnated by the Spirit of God, which resulted in Jesus' having a human mother and a divine father; this ensured the truth of his two natures. The difficulty with this interpretation, however, lies partly in the fact that nowhere in scripture is the Spirit's action that "comes upon" and "overshadows" a person analogous to sexual intercourse. Rather, these verbs indicate the presence of God who empowers and protects:

• *Eperchesthai* ("come upon") in Greek literally signifies the coming and going of persons or things such as ships. This rootedness in physical movement in space equips the word to function figuratively to point to the intangible approach of the living God. Carrying the notion of onrushing, overpowering vitality, it tells of divine presence on the move creating something new. A prime example is Jesus' saying in Acts that assures his disciples after his resurrection, "You will receive power when the Holy Spirit has *come upon* you" (Acts 1:8). When this does indeed happen, the women and men of his circle are empowered to preach the good news to the ends of the earth. This same sense of empowerment is well attested in the Hebrew Bible. After Samuel's anointing, "the Spirit of the Lord *came mightily upon* David from that day forward," beginning his march toward kingship (1 Sam. 16:13). Isaiah foretells devastation "until the Spirit *comes upon* us from on high," when a period of blessed refreshment will begin (Isa. 32:15). These and other biblical examples make clear that the Spirit "coming upon" someone is not sexual but creatively empowering in a broader sense. It connotes the approach of the power of God in a decisively new way.

• *Episkiazein* ("overshadow") in Greek literally means to cast a shadow on something. In contemporary Western parlance this may have a negative, ominous ring. In the Middle East, however, where the sun is so strong it can fry your brains, the cooling shadow of a little tree or even the wall of a building is much appreciated. When used in scripture with reference to God, "overshadowing" thus has the positive meaning of manifesting powerful divine protection over a person or even the whole people. The word is often coupled with concrete images such as a moving cloud or sheltering wings under whose shadow persons find refuge, figurative ways of speaking about God's protection from harm. John Calvin thought the cloud was a particularly "elegant metaphor" for divine presence insofar as it conceals as much as it reveals, covering over divine glory with a haze of brilliance. With this nuance, the overshadowing cloud resonates with allusions to the *Shekinah,* the indwelling, saving presence of the Holy One in later rabbinic writings.

Two other instances closely parallel this verb's meaning in the annunciation text. In the exodus story a cloud settles on the tent of meeting that Moses pitched in the desert: "the cloud *overshadowed* it and the glory of the Lord filled the tabernacle" (Exod. 40:34ff.). When the cloud rose, the people followed it and trekked on; when it settled down on the tabernacle, they rested. Casting a shadow by day, shot through with fire at night, "the movement of the cloud directs the journey toward freedom." What is being spoken of here is the presence of God. Signified by the cloud, this presence protects, refreshes, directs, liberates. Again, all three Synoptic Gospels use the same verb in their account of Jesus' transfiguration: "Then a cloud *overshadowed* them, and from the cloud there came a voice . . ." (Mark 9:7; Matt. 17:5; Luke 9:34). As in the Sinai story, the action of the cloud, itself a metaphor of divine presence, brings God close to the scene with gracious, redemptive intent. The voice speaks the same message about Jesus' being the Son of God as was already heard at the baptism, and the two scenes are parallel. The Spirit descends like a dove, the cloud of glory overshadows, and Jesus' messianic identity is revealed.

Overshadowing, then, always means the Spirit of God drawing near and passing by to save and protect. Given this usage, given that neither in secular nor religious language does the word ever function as a euphemism for sexual intercourse, it is clear that the Holy Spirit's overshadowing Mary in the annunciation story is, as Carsten Colpe insists, "the opposite of human procreation." What is being described is not a god impregnating a mortal woman such as occurs in Hellenistic stories of sacred marriage. Luke does not mean that God acts as a substitute male sexual partner. Indeed, Paul can write of Isaac that he was "the child who was born according to the Spirit" (Gal. 4:29) without implying that Abraham's sexual paternity was absent. As the ecumenical authors of *Mary in the New Testament* teach, "the overshadowing of 1:35 has no sexual implication." Rather, the term comes from a tradition "where no sexual import is possible. God is not a sexual partner but a creative power in the begetting of Jesus." Remembering the female imagery used in scripture of the Holy Spirit—*rûaḥ,* mother, Sophia—further strengthens this philological insight. The Spirit does not mate with Mary.

Hence, the angel does not answer Mary's objection with a satisfactory description of the mechanics of "how shall this be." Joseph Fitzmyer's judgment about what happened historically is the baseline from which all theologizing should proceed: "What really happened? We shall never know." In view of the religious meaning of Mary's pregnancy, however, we know a great deal. The text declares that the creative presence of God's Spirit will be with her. As Schaberg explains, "What is the essence of this second angelic response? It is this: You should trust; you will be empowered and protected by God. The reversal of Elizabeth's humiliation shows that nothing is impossible for God." Recall how in the opening scene in Genesis, the Spirit of God blows like a mighty wind over the dark waters and the world came into being. Just so, in this new moment of the renewal of creation, the Spirit is on the move again. Recall, furthermore, the Easter proclamation that it is by the Spirit that Jesus is raised from the dead and made Son of God in power. Just so, the same life-giving Spirit creates him as Son of God at his conception. The point for our remembering here is that both in its structure as a commissioning story and in its metaphors of the Spirit's coming upon and overshadowing, this scene with its primary christological interest is a theophany. It places this woman in deep, attentive relation to the Spirit of God. Mary belongs in the company of those whom Spirit-Sophia approaches: "From generation to generation she enters into holy souls and makes them friends of God and prophets" (Wis. 7:27). We do not have access to Mary's religious experience, but can simply say that by the power of the Spirit she encountered the mystery of the living God, the gracious God of her life, the saving Wisdom of her people. In that encounter, the die was cast for the coming of the Messiah.

Consent

All of this takes place as a result of God's free initiative. As always in biblical portrayals of divine interaction with human beings, divine freedom does not override created freedom but waits upon our free response, which, in a theology of grace, God has already made possible. Hearing the divine call, Mary decides to say yes. Casting her lot with the future, she responds with courage and, as the next scene of the visitation will show, with joy and prophecy to this unexpected call: "And Mary said, 'Behold the handmaid of the Lord. Be it done to me according to your word.'" Here Luke innovates by adding

Mary's verbal consent as a sixth, climactic element to the literary structure of the announcement story, whose design normally has five points whether used for prophetic commissioning or foretelling birth. "In none of the twenty-seven Hebrew Bible commissionings, none of the ten nonbiblical accounts, none of the fifteen other commissionings in Luke-Acts, and none of the nine other New Testament commissionings . . . are the commissioned ones depicted as assenting verbally and directly to their commission," Schaberg analyzes. Luke's innovation is meant to underscore Mary's conscious and active faith as one who hears the word of God and keeps it. Here I am. *Fiat.* Her stance is one that affirms her own identity in the act of radical trust in God, based on a bedrock conviction that God is faithful. Over the centuries many persons have understood and been inspired by this.

In our day, however, Luke's intention is subverted by the language of slavery. In the original Greek of the gospels the word *doulē,* which is usually translated "handmaid," literally means female slave girl; *kyriou* means literally "master" or "lord." The relationship signified by this phrase "handmaid of the Lord" is thus enormously problematic in feminist and womanist theology. As we already criticized, centuries of patriarchal interpretation have labeled Mary's response as submissive obedience and have held up this stance as the proper ideal for all women in relation to men, a view antithetical to women's hopes for their own human dignity. The bias involved becomes clearer by contrast, as Luise Schottroff points out: when Paul uses *doulos* to describe himself (Rom. 1:1), interpreters think of ministry and office rather than of humble obedience. Traditional demands for conformity to patriarchal order and for obedience to male religious authority figures, be they God, husband, or priest, make women shudder before this text and reject it as dangerous to physical and psychological health as well as to a liberating spirituality.

One might argue to the contrary that obedience, which word in fact does *not* appear in the text, comes from the Latin *ob-audire*, meaning "to listen," in this case to listen to the word of God. One might also point out that Luke is here depicting Mary as the ideal disciple, whose chief characteristic is hearing the word of God and keeping it, doing it, acting upon it, responding to it, this being the model for both women and men disciples without distinction. Again, one might take *doulē* in its most literal meaning, a female slave, connect it with the Pentecost story where Mary also appears, and interpret it as an instance of the glorious freedom of the last days when God's Spirit will be poured out upon all flesh, yes, "even upon my slaves, both men and women, in those days I will pour out my Spirit, and they shall prophesy" (Acts 2:18, citing Joel 2:28–32). This interpretation has the advantage of showing how the advent of the Spirit lifts up the lowly, reverses their low estate, unseals their lips, and empowers them to prophesy. Again, one may even translate the term *doulē* not as handmaid or female slave but as the generic "servant," thereby linking Mary to the whole lineage of distinguished faithful servants of God including Abraham and Moses, Deborah and Hannah, culminating with the Servant of Yahweh in Isaiah. But helpful though such moves may be, they do not get at the root of the problem, which is the master–slave relationship, now totally abhorrent in human society and no longer suitable as a metaphor for relationship to God, certainly not in feminist theological understanding. African American women who write theology out of the heritage of slavery and subsequent domestic servitude stress this repugnance even more strongly in unmistakable terms. Slavery is an unjust, sinful situation. It makes people into objects owned by others, denigrating their dignity as human persons. In the case of slave women, their masters have the right not only to their labor but to their bodies, making them into tools of production and reproduction at the master's wish. In such circumstances the Spirit groans with the cries of the oppressed, prompting persons not to obey but to resist, using all their wiles.

Rather than defending this master–slave metaphor as written by Luke in a world where it was not questioned, a more satisfying strategy allows us to criticize it and then look for the liberating reality at the core of Mary's response. Very carefully we peel off the layers of saccharine humility and forced subordination. This young peasant girl discerns the voice of God in her life commissioning her to a momentous task. Exercising independent thought and action, she asks questions, takes counsel with her own soul. In a self-determining act of personal autonomy, she decides to go for it. This is her choice and it changes her life. A woman of Spirit, she embarks on the task of partnering God in the work of redemption. African American theologian Diana Hayes describes Mary's action here as one of "outrageous authority"; standing alone, she yet had enough faith in herself and in her God to say a powerful and prophetic yes. From a Latin American viewpoint, Ana María Bidegain argues that far from signifying "self-denial, passivity, and submission as the essential attributes of women," Mary's consent is a free act of self-bestowal for the purpose of co-creating a new world. In this light, "Mary's humility consists in the daring to accept the monumental undertaking proposed to her by God"; her consent is a free and responsible act, "not the yes of self-denial." In consort with other Asian thinkers, Chung Hyun Kyung emphasizes the risk this decision involved. Mary's initial hesitation was well founded, for her choice turned her world upside down. She was not a heroic superwoman but a village woman of the people, albeit one who was attentive to God's calling, and this calling drew her from her own private safety. "With fear and trembling she takes the risk of participating in God's plan out of her vision of redeemed humanity. . . . Jesus was born through the body of this woman, a liberated, mature woman, who had a mind and will of her own, capable of self-determination and perseverance in her decisions."

Women note that in this scene God speaks directly to Mary, the message not being mediated through her father, betrothed spouse, or priest. In addition, she does not turn to any male authority figure either to be advised or to seek permission regarding what is to be done. Indeed, the setting is not the temple with its priestly cult, where Zechariah earlier received his announcement, but her own lay, female space, in the village. While still operating within a patriarchal text, she is portrayed in terms of her relationship to God independent of men's control, a stance that in itself undermines patriarchal ideology. Poet Kathleen Norris notes how in this scene Mary finds her voice, rather than losing it. Like any prophet, she asserts herself before God saying, "Here am I." This picture of a young woman courageously committing herself in turn "may provide an excellent means of conveying to girls that there is something in them that no man can touch; that belongs only to them, and to God."

Existentially, Mary's response carries with it a fundamental definition of her personhood. Facing a critical choice, she sums herself up "in one of those great self-constituting decisions that give shape to a human life." In a by now classic analysis of the human situation, Valerie Saiving observed that, conditioned as we are by patriarchy, the traditional "temptations of woman *as woman* are not the same as the temptations of man *as man.*" Unlike men, women experience temptations that "have a quality which can never be encompassed by such terms as 'pride' and 'will-to-power.' They are better suggested by . . . underdevelopment or negation of the self." Drifting, overdependence on the judgment of others, and self-sacrificing in order to please are but a few examples of feminine traps. The memory that this young woman's decision is not a passive, timid reaction but a free and autonomous act encourages and endorses women's efforts to take responsibility for their own lives. The courage of her decision vis-à-vis the Holy One is at the same time an assent to the totality of herself. Remembering Mary's *fiat* in this light, Dutch theologian Catharina Halkes writes that far from the passivity imposed on women by a patriarchal society and church, Mary's stance is one of "utmost attentiveness and the creativity which flows from it, based on a listening life." Far from being the "proper" attitude of a slave girl, such a grasp of oneself in the world forges a way of integrity in the midst of society's dissipating demands. In the paradigmatic commissioning narrative of the annunciation, encountering God's redemptive grace and empowered by the Spirit, Mary was not *forced* to bear the Messiah. Acting as a responsible moral agent, she made her own choice.

The annunciation is a faith event. Dramatically, this poor, unconventional peasant woman's free and autonomous answer opens a new chapter in the history of God with the world. "It is Mary's faith that makes possible God's entrance into history," writes Ruether, in the sense that henceforth God will be at home in the flesh of the world in a new way. Brazilian theologians Ivone Gebara and María Clara Bingemer note that annunciations keep on happening, bringing into the ordinariness of life a message of God's gracious care and desire to repair the world. Touching the root of our humanity, these messages reveal hidden possibilities within the limits of our existence, revive our hope in the midst of struggle, and summon our energies for creative action. Seen in this light the particulars of Mary's call, unique in that only one woman conceives and delivers Jesus, illuminate the fundamental dynamic of everyone's vocation through the ages. The Holy One calls all people, indeed all women, and gifts them for their own task in the ongoing history of grace. In the midst of family, work, and social life in village, suburb, and city, it begins with an encounter in the solitude of the heart before God: everywoman, the voice, the call, the courageous response, in the context of a world struggling for life.

The disclosive power of the structure of the annunciation story, along with its central elements of the Spirit's presence and the woman's response, place Miriam of Nazareth in the company of all ancestors in the faith who heard the word of God and responded with courageous love. Now like Abraham, she sets out in faith, not knowing where she is going. Now like Sarah, she receives power to conceive by this faith, considering the One who promised to be worthy of her trust. Listening to the Spirit, rising to the immense possibilities of her call, she walks by faith in the integrity of her own person. Inspired by Spirit-Sophia, women who make their own decisions before God claim her into their circle.

Visitation: Joy in the Revolution of God

Luke 1:39–56

FRESH FROM HER ENCOUNTER with the angel, "Mary arose and went with haste into the hill country" to visit her kinswoman Elizabeth, herself swelling with a pregnancy in her old age. Filled with the Spirit, both women burst into glorious speech. Elizabeth salutes Mary, who in turn sings out a prophetic song of praise to God. Known as the Magnificat from its opening word in Latin translation, this canticle can barely contain her joy over the liberation coming to fruition in herself and the world through the creative power of the Spirit. As noted earlier, classical mariology rarely dealt with this prayer. Its radical depiction of Mary's no to oppression completes her earlier yes to solidarity with the project of the reign of God. By sealing this page of scripture, such theology managed to suppress the portrait of Mary as a prophet and to forestall the upheaval that would ensue from oppressed peoples, including women, taking a similar stance. Yet as Schaberg rightly describes, "the Magnificat is the great New Testament song of liberation—personal and social, moral and economic—a revolutionary document of intense conflict and victory. It praises God's actions on behalf of the speaker, which are paradigmatic of all of God's actions on behalf of marginal and exploited people." Evoking the powerful memory of God's deliverance of enslaved Israel from Egypt, it praises God's continuing actions throughout history to redeem the lowly, including the speaker herself and all marginal and exploited people. Rooted in Jewish tradition, Mary stands as the singer of the song of justice of the coming messianic age. Tracing the contours of this scene and its theology from a critical biblical and feminist perspective places a dazzling, unmistakably prophetic tile in the mosaic of the critical remembrance of Mary.

Early church writers already interpreted this scene with a prophetic gloss. Ambrose saw in Mary's hurried journey through the hill country of Judea an analogy to the church's stride across the hills of centuries. He connected both travelers to the itinerant prophet of glad tidings depicted by Isaiah who wrote, "How beautiful upon the mountains are the feet of the messenger who announces peace, who brings good news, who announces salvation" (Isa. 52:7). Ambrose then exhorts, "Watch Mary, my children, for the word uttered prophetically of the church applies also to her: 'How beautiful thy sandaled steps, O generous maid!' Yes, generous and beautiful indeed are the church's steps as she goes to announce her gospel of joy: lovely the feet of Mary and the church." Irenaeus, after showing how Christ became a human being so that human beings might become children of God, depicts Mary's song leading the way for the church's response: "Therefore Mary rejoiced, and speaking prophetically in the church's name she said, 'My soul magnifies the Lord.'" Finding Mary the prophet in this text thus develops an ancient tradition. In our day new dimensions emerge when this text is read with biblical scholarship through women's eyes.

Two Women Meeting

First, the encounter. The house is Zechariah's but he has been struck dumb. No other men are around. Such quieting of the male voice is highly unusual in scripture. Into this spacious silence two women's voices resound, one praising the other and both praising God. This is a rare biblical vignette of a conversation between two women. Despite the overall andro-centric literary context, this story is told in an entirely gyno-centric manner. The outpouring of the Spirit on Elizabeth and Mary happens in traditionally female domestic space. Women are the actors who hold center stage; women are the speakers who powerfully convey the resounding good news; women themselves embody the mercy of God which they prophetically proclaim. And they do so in the context of meeting and affirming one another.

Both personal and political insights weave their threads into the texture of this scene. In *Just a Sister Away*, African American biblical scholar Renita Weems notes how pregnant women have an almost physical need for the company of others in the same condition to share their fears, find courage, express hopes, and learn practical wisdom about how their bodies are changing. Being singled out as mothers of redemption made Elizabeth and Mary need each other for this and much more. Having resigned herself to living with disappointment over never having had a child, Elizabeth now has to deal with an "unexpected blessing." Mary in turn has to figure out how to live with a blessing that causes more problems than it solves. How explain this to Joseph? This was not how she had planned her life. Each needed to talk with another woman who knew what it meant to grapple with God's intentions. Their mutual encouragement enabled them to go forward with more confidence and joy despite the struggle that still faced them.

Focusing on "the politics of meeting," Tina Pippin sees that by connecting with each other, these two women are empowered to speak with prophetic voices. They meet, and the force of their meeting leads them to proclaim in the midst of their history that God blesses the lowly and overthrows oppressive institutions. Through their discourse they image power by setting forth the political meaning of their pregnancies, namely, hope for the dispossessed people of Israel. Here is a rare glimpse of female reproductive power as both physically nurturing and politically revolutionary. "The two pregnant women beat the drum of God's world revolution" (Luise Schottroff), starting with the option for debased women and then including all the starving, powerless, and oppressed. A pregnant woman is not the usual image that comes to mind when one thinks of a prophet, yet here are two such spirit-filled pregnant prophets crying out in joy, warning, and hope for the future. Clearly this is a picture of Mary that is the complete opposite of the passive, humble handmaid of the patriarchal imagination. Susan Ross envisions yet another way this text is dangerous: it portrays women looking to each other for validation of their authority rather than to men. This experience of female solidarity is unequaled in its ability to support women's struggles for equal justice and care, for themselves and for others. Whether one sees Elizabeth and Mary as "women of Spirit birthing hope," or as the Spirit-approved "pregnant crone and the unmarried, pregnant bride suspected of adultery" (Barbara Reid), their meeting is powerful and potentially empowering. It brings the theme of women's solidarity and mutual female empowerment into the mosaic of the memory of Mary.

Elizabeth's Song

This older woman had been faithfully walking in the way of God for many long years. Luke draws her portrait using the paint of the Hebrew scripture's barren matriarch tradition, especially the stories of Sarah, Rebekah, Rachel, Samson's mother, and Hannah, and the symbol of the barren Jerusalem. The parameters of this tradition are patriarchal: a woman's worth resides in her ability to bear sons for her husband and her people. Rooted in their time and place, the biblical writers seem unable to envision any other kind of world, such as one where women would exercise other social functions and equal value would be given to the birth of daughters. Within their own limited context, however, they signal God's compassionate vindication of the lowly with stories of humiliated women being blessed by conceiving and bearing a son. Long childless but called righteous nevertheless, Elizabeth lives such a story. In the annunciation, her pregnancy has already been used as a sign to encourage Mary at her calling. Now, "filled with the Holy Spirit," she greets the younger woman with exuberant blessing.

Seeing deep wisdom in this passage of one woman blessing another, Barbara Reid calls attention to the back story. Earlier when Elizabeth had first conceived she said, "So has the Lord done for me" (Luke 1:24). Compared to her husband's difficult, doubting dialogue with the angel, it is striking how easily she recognizes the grace of God coming into her life. A long life of attentiveness to the Spirit enables her to see that this child is not a gift for Zechariah or her people alone, but signifies God's gracious regard of herself as a loved and valuable person: "so has the Lord done for *me*." Then, sequestered for six months "alone with God and her silent husband," she nurtures the life within her while contemplating the divine compassion she is experiencing. Elizabeth names the grace in her own life so well that when Mary comes calling, she is prepared to recognize and name the grace of another (Mary Catherine Hilkert). Her experience of God's fidelity is used to give confidence to another:

> Blessed are you among women, and blessed is the fruit of your womb. And why is this granted me, that the mother of my Lord should come to me? For behold, when the voice of your greeting came to my ears, the babe in my womb leaped for joy. And blessed is she who believed that there would be a fulfillment of what was spoken to her from the Lord.

Luke does not give Elizabeth the title of prophet, but "filled with the Holy Spirit" she functions like one. She blesses Mary as a woman in her own right first, then her child, then her faith. Her words echo the praise addressed to other women famous in Israelite history who have helped to deliver God's people from peril. When Jael dispatches an enemy of the people, the prophet Deborah utters, "Most blessed be Jael among women" (Judg. 5:24). After Judith's spectacular defeat of the enemy general, Uzziah praises her, "O daughter, you are blessed by the Most High God above all other women on the earth" (Jdt. 13:18). The scholars of *Mary in the New Testament* caution that the fact such blessings have been invoked upon other women "prevents us from taking it too absolutely, as if it meant that Mary was the most blessed woman who ever lived." The "alone of all her sex" syndrome cannot be inferred from this verse, taken in context. Rather, Elizabeth's exuberant praise shouted with unrestrained joy joins Mary to solidarity with a long heritage of women whose creative action, undertaken in the power of the Spirit, brings liberation in

God's name. Moreover, this blessing weds her historic pregnancy to her faith, again depicting her as someone who hears the word of God and acts upon it even in her own body.

Mary remained with Elizabeth for about three months. During that time before the birth of John, Zechariah remains silent. Luke does not depict their time together, but in women's reflection Elizabeth takes Mary in and nurtures her, affirms her calling, nourishes her confidence. Together they chart the changes taking place in their bodies and affirm the grace in their own and each other's lives. Their gladness hails the advent of the messianic age. The support they share with each other enables them to mother the next generation of prophets, the Precursor and the Savior of the world. On balance, the figure of Elizabeth stands as a moving embodiment of the wisdom and care that older women can offer younger ones, who, brave as they are, are just starting out on their journey through life. A Spirit-filled woman, she exudes blessing on others. Preceding Mary in childbirth and in theologizing, her presence assures the younger woman that she does not face the uncertain future alone. Her mature experience sustains the new venture. What emerges with undoubted clarity from their interaction is women's ability to interpret God's word for other women.

Mary's Song

Swelling with new life by the power of the Spirit and affirmed by her kinswoman, Mary sings the Magnificat, a canticle that joyfully proclaims God's gracious, effective compassion at the advent of the messianic age. It should be noted at the outset that as the longest passage put on the lips of any female speaker in the New Testament, this is the most any woman gets to say. Other women have life-changing visions of angels, most significantly at the empty tomb on Easter morning, but while we are told that they proclaim the good news, we unfortunately do not get to hear their own words. The cadences of this canticle stand in righteous criticism against such scriptural silencing of "the lowly." While Luke may silence the voice of Mary Magdalene, Joanna, and others, our interpretation today reads against his intent, to find in Mary's song a protest against the suppression of women's voices and a spark for their prophetic speech. Following the logic of her praise, who can dare tell women they cannot speak?

> And Mary said:
> "My soul magnifies the Lord,
> and my spirit rejoices in God my Savior,
> for he has looked with favor on the lowliness of his
>   handmaid.
> For behold, henceforth all generations will call me
>   blessed,
> for the One who is mighty has done great things for me,
> and holy is his name.
> And his mercy is from generation to generation on
>   those who fear him.
> He has shown strength with his arm;
> he has scattered the proud in the imagination of their
>   hearts;
> he has put down the mighty from their thrones,
> and exalted those of low degree;
> he has filled the hungry with good things,
> and the rich he has sent empty away.
> He has helped his servant Israel,
> in remembrance of his mercy,
> according to the promise he made to our ancestors,
> to Abraham and to his posterity forever.

The Galilean woman who proclaims this canticle stands in the long Jewish tradition of female singers from Miriam with her tambourine (Exod. 15:2–21) to Deborah (Judg. 5:1–31), Hannah (1 Sam. 2:1–10), and Judith (Jdt. 16:1–17), who also sang dangerous songs of salvation. Their songs are psalms of thanksgiving, victory songs of the oppressed. In particular, the song's form and even whole phrases are explicitly modeled on the canticle of Hannah in the book of Samuel. From Hannah's opening lines, "My heart exults in the Lord; my strength is exalted in my God," to her prophetic verses, "The bows of the mighty are broken, but the feeble gird on strength; those who were full have hired themselves out for bread, but those who were hungry are fat with spoil," the parallelism links both women in their vocal response to the peculiar mercy of Israel's God, who graciously chooses to be in solidarity with those who suffer and are of no account in order to heal, redeem, and liberate.

Composed according to the overall structure of a thanksgiving psalm, which first praises God and then lists the reasons for gratitude, the Magnificat has two main stanzas or strophes. The first praises divine mercy to the speaker and the second reflects the Holy One's victorious deeds for the oppressed community. Far from being separate pieces, the two stanzas are linked theologically by a profound sense of God's faithful compassion, existentially by the atmosphere of joy that results in the lives of the liberated, and socially by virtue of the speaker Mary's being herself a member of the oppressed people who experience redemption. The unity in distinction of the two stanzas, one praising God with deep personal love and the other proclaiming God's justice, can be seen to reflect a way of life basic to Jewish and Christian traditions: love of God and love of neighbor in gospel terms, or spirituality and social justice according to the prophets, or contemplation and action in the tenets of traditional spirituality, or mysticism and resistance in the terms of contemporary theology. By attending to the way this canticle resonates with the rich biblical traditions that celebrate God's liberation, we add the prophetic Mary, now singing her song of salvation, to our mosaic.

1. God's mercy to the peasant woman: The canticle begins with a poor woman's cry of joy. Mary's soul magnifies the Lord and her spirit rejoices in "God my Savior." This lyric mood, so characteristic of intimate experience of relationship with God, pervades the Jewish biblical tradition. The psalmist sings: "Then my soul shall rejoice in the Lord, exulting in his deliverance" (Ps. 35:9); the prophet Isaiah encourages: "This is the Lord for whom we have waited; let us be glad and rejoice in his salvation" (Isa. 25:9); even the natural world is caught up in the gladness: "Let all the earth cry out to God with joy" (Ps. 66:1). What does it mean to rejoice in God your Savior? This is not a superficial joy but is written against the whole canvas of the world's pain. It is messianic joy, paschal joy, aware of the struggle unto death yet hopeful that the great "nevertheless" of God leads to life. In the midst of suffering and turmoil, the sense of divine presence in compassionate care offers strength, leading one to be glad that God is great. Mary *magnifies* God her Savior, which in formal Elizabethan English means to celebrate the greatness, or sing and dance in praise of the goodness of someone wonderful. Her soul and her spirit do this, meaning her whole self, her whole being, with body, mind, and strength. Hers are not the words of half-hearted appreciation. She is caught up, feels herself lifted up into God's good and gracious will. With a foretaste of eschatological delight, she breaks forth in praise and singing.

Mary's song is the prayer of a poor woman. She proclaims

God's greatness with her whole being because the Holy One of Israel, regarding her low estate, has done great things for her. The term for lowliness, *tapeinōsis* in Greek, describes misery, pain, persecution, and oppression. In Genesis it describes the situation in the wilderness of the escaping slave woman Hagar, whom God heeds (Gen. 16:11); in the exodus story it describes the severe affliction from which God delivers the people (Exod. 3:7). Mary's self-characterization as lowly is not a metaphor for spiritual humility but is based on her actual social position. Young, female, a member of a people subjected to economic exploitation by powerful ruling groups, afflicted by outbreaks of violence, she belongs to the semantic domain of the poor in Luke's gospel, a group given a negative valuation by worldly powers. Yet it is to precisely such a woman that the call has come to partner God in the great work of redemption. Just such a woman will mother the Messiah because God has regarded her, has turned the divine countenance toward her and let divine pleasure shine upon her. It is not just that God often chooses unconventional people for a task, not just that Mary is among the inconsequential poor of the earth, like unlettered women in any poor village on this planet. It is the combination that is revolutionary: God has regarded *her* precisely as a lowly woman. Her favored status, declared by Gabriel, Elizabeth, and now herself, results from God's surprising and gracious initiative. Rejoicing follows. Here the background picture of a poor, first-century Galilean peasant woman living in occupied territory, struggling for survival and dignity against victimization, imbued with Jewish faith, aptly coalesces with this biblical portrait of Mary, singer of the song of justice in the name of God.

In his commentary on this canticle, Martin Luther sought

to place its sentiments squarely at the center of the church's life. Mary's song gives all of us confidence in God's grace, he teaches, for despite our lowliness God has a "hearty desire" to do great things for us too. What we need is faith, trusting in God as Mary did with "her whole life and being, mind and strength." Then we will be caught up in God's good and gracious will, which operates with kindness, mercy, justice, and righteousness. True, this always involves a reversal of values, "and the mightier you are, the more must you fear; the lowlier you are, the more must you take comfort." But just as the Spirit overshadowed Mary, inspiring her joy and fortitude, so too the Spirit imbues us every day with rich and abundant grace to follow our own calling. The important thing to remember is that Mary had confidence in God, finding in God her Savior a wellspring of joy and comfort. "Thus we too should do; that would be to sing a right Magnificat."

2. God's mercy to the oppressed people: What begins as praise for divine loving-kindness toward a marginalized and oppressed woman grows in amplitude to include all the poor of the world. The second strophe of the Magnificat articulates the great biblical theme of reversal where lowly groups of people are defended by God while the arrogant end up losers. All through scripture the revelatory experience of the character of God who liberated the Hebrew slaves from bondage finds ongoing expression in texts that praise divine redemptive care for the lost. In the psalms and the prophets, the Holy One of Israel protects, defends, saves, and rescues these "nobodies," adorning them with victory and life in the face of despair. Proclaiming the Magnificat, Mary continues this deep stream of Jewish faith in the context of the advent of the Messiah, now taking shape within her. The approach of the

reign of God will disturb the order of the world run by the arrogant, the hard of heart, the oppressor. Through God's action, the social hierarchy of wealth and poverty, power and subjugation, is to be turned upside down. Jubilation breaks out as the proud are scattered and the mighty are pulled from their thrones while the lowly are exalted and mercy in the form of food fills the bellies of the hungry. All will be well, and all manner of thing will be well, because God's mercy, pledged in covenant love, is faithful through every generation.

In all the gospels, Jesus preaches and acts out this vital message of reversal. The Asian women theologians at the Singapore Conference note with unassailable logic that "with the singer of the Magnificat as his mother, it should not surprise us that Jesus' first words in Luke's account of his public ministry are also a mandate for radical change." The beatitudes encapsulate this message in especially dramatic form: "Happy are you poor . . . you who hunger now . . . you who weep now. . . . But woe to you rich . . . who are full now . . . who laugh now" (Luke 6:20–26). Through his own death and resurrection this same reversal is embodied in Jesus himself, who becomes the mother lode of God's life-giving mercy for the world. By placing the Magnificat on the lips of Mary, Luke depicts her as the spokeswoman for God's redemptive justice, which will be such a part of the gospel. She proclaims the good news by anticipation, and she does so as a Jewish woman whose consciousness is deeply rooted in the heritage and wisdom of the strong women of Israel. Knowledgeable about the liberating traditions of her own people and trumpeting them with "tough authority," this friend of God stands as a prophet of the coming age. "The song of Mary is the oldest Advent hymn," preached Dietrich Bonhoeffer, the German theologian killed by the Nazis:

It is at once the most passionate, the wildest, one might even say the most revolutionary Advent hymn ever sung. This is not the gentle, tender, dreamy Mary whom we sometimes see in paintings; this is the passionate, surrendered, proud, enthusiastic Mary who speaks out here. This song has none of the sweet, nostalgic, or even playful tones of some of our Christmas carols. It is instead a hard, strong, inexorable song about collapsing thrones and humbled lords of this world, about the power of God and the powerlessness of humankind. These are the tones of the women prophets of the Old Testament that now come to life in Mary's mouth.

A dispute about the origin of this canticle sheds light on the material significance of this second strophe. Based on its form and religious content, some biblical scholars think that the song was written by the early church in Jerusalem. Its christology, which interprets Jesus as the Davidic Messiah, has Jewish overtones, and its piety is redolent of the prayer of the *anawim*, a term meaning "poor ones." Raymond Brown argues forcefully that the early church in Jerusalem saw themselves as *anawim*, combining as they did material poverty with temple piety. Along with other canticles in Luke's infancy narrative uttered by Zechariah and Simeon, he believes, the Magnificat formed part of the "hymn book" of this Jerusalem community described at the beginning of Acts. For Luke to place the song on Mary's lips, adding the verse about God's regard for his lowly handmaid, is artistically and theologically apt, given her Jewish faith, her material poverty, and her probable participation in this post-resurrection community of disciples.

To the contrary, other scholars think that the milieu in which the Magnificat originated was not the religious life of the Jerusalem community but the political struggle of the people of Palestine against their oppressors. The song portrays intense conflict. The six central verbs that describe God's help to Israel denote forceful action: show strength, scatter, pull down, lift up, fill up, send away. There are close parallels between this hymn and other Jewish hymns from the period of arduous resistance to imperial rule, including the Qumran *War Scroll* and hymns celebrating the victory of the Maccabees (today's feast of Hanukkah). Richard Horsley argues that the core subject of the song is God's revolutionary overthrow of the established governing authorities who are squeezing the life out of the people, a view made even more cogent when we recognize that "the words and phrases used throughout the Magnificat are taken from and vividly recall the whole tradition of victory songs and hymns of praise celebrating God's victorious liberation of the people of Israel from their oppressive enemies." Correlatively, there are no *anawim* as a spiritual group; the term applies to the people generally, caught in bad and worsening socioeconomic conditions.

It may be that both views are right in their own way. The Jerusalem community may have taken a preexisting victory hymn already in circulation and adapted it for their own use. Brown notes, furthermore, that the first followers of Jesus were Galileans; that Galilee was the spawning ground of first-century revolts against repressive Roman occupation and the heavy tax burden it laid on people's backs; and that there was real poverty among those who became the nucleus of the post-resurrection church. In this setting, the spiritual themes of the Magnificat have real economic and political resonance as the song declares that these poor people are ultimately the blessed ones, not the mighty and the rich who oppress them.

The value of this debate lies in the way it alerts us to the presence of a memory that is truly dangerous. The history of interpretation contains many instances of thinkers who opt to spiritualize this text, to take away its political teeth, to blunt its radical tone by appeal to the eschatological reversal promised for the last day. Rooted in the biblical heritage of Palestinian Jewish society, however, the song's provenance makes clear that it is a revolutionary song of salvation whose concrete social, economic, and political dimensions cannot be blunted. People are hungry because of triple monies being exacted for empire, client-king, and temple. The lowly are being crushed because of the mighty on their thrones in Rome and their deputies in the provinces. Now, with the nearness of the messianic age, a new social order of justice and plenty is at hand. Like the beatitudes Jesus proclaims for the poor and brokenhearted, Mary's canticle praises God for the kind of salvation that involves concrete transformations.

People in need in every society hear a blessing in this canticle. The battered woman, the single parent without resources, those without food on the table or without even a table, the homeless family, the young abandoned to their own devices, the old who are discarded—all who are subjected to social contempt are encompassed in the hope Mary proclaims. Working amid the poor in India, R. J. Raja reflects that Mary portrays the God of Israel, who will "not stop short of subverting all satanic structures of oppression, inhuman establishments of inequality, and systems which generate slavery and non-freedom," including those that debase people on account of their birth, caste, sex, creed, color, religion, tenets, weakness, and poverty. It is precisely in this way that God is established as Savior of the people in the face of human degradation. The church in Latin America more than any other is responsible for hearing this proclamation of hope in a newly refreshed way. The Magnificat's message is so subversive that for a period during the 1980s the government of Guatemala banned its public recitation. Seeing the central point of this song to be the assertion of the holiness of God, Peruvian Gustavo Gutiérrez argues, "Any exegesis is fruitless that attempts to tone down what Mary's song tells us about preferential love of God for the lowly and the abused, and about the transformation of history that God's loving will implies."

This message will not appeal to those who are satisfied with the ways things are. It will also be ignored by those who seek to restore intact some past epoch in the history of culture or religion. Even affluent people of good will have difficulty dealing with its shocking, revolutionary ring. Doesn't God love everyone? Indeed yes, but in an unjust world, the form this universal love takes differs according to circumstance. The language of this canticle makes clear that divine love is particularly on the side of those whose dignity must be recovered. God protects the poor, noticing their tears, while challenging the comfortable and the proud to conversion, to genuine discipleship, even at the loss of their own comfort. The divine intent is not to take revenge and so create a new order of injustice but to build up a community of sisters and brothers marked by human dignity and mutual regard. Only thus is the coming reign of God rendered genuinely historical. Addressing his economically privileged compatriots, John Haught offers a valuable insight. For those who have little, for the destitute and dispossessed, for the wretched of the Earth, for the *anawim* of Yahweh, he writes, there remains only the ever-coming God of the future to sustain their lives and aspirations. "A major part of the message of prophetic religion is that the dreams that arise among the poor are not naive illusions but compelling clues to the nature of the real. . . . Perhaps only by allowing our own lives to be integrated into the horizon of their dreams and expectations, that is, by our own solidarity with victims, can we too make ourselves vulnerable to the power of the future." Rather than legitimate or ignore the miserable circumstances of the afflicted, those who are affluent need to dream with the poor the dream of God's future that their suffering opens up, and thus be transformed themselves. For both poor and affluent, the Magnificat is a vehicle of that dream.

3. Both stanzas together. This is a profoundly theocentric canticle, centering the singer on God's gracious goodness for personal and communal reasons. In Edward Schillebeeckx's inimitable phrase, it is a "toast to our God," offered in jubilant thanksgiving in the midst of the tragic history of the world. The point for our remembering is that Mary not only sings of God's liberating transformation of the social order in redemptive acts of mercy, but she herself embodies the oppressed people, who have been exalted through God's compassionate action. Like those enumerated in her song, she occupies a position of poverty and powerlessness in her society, and does so with the added oppression that accrues to being a woman of little account. Hence her song puts her in solidarity with other women who strive for life: "Mary appears in its strains no longer as the sweet mother of traditional piety. She is now made to speak in concert with the oppressed wives and the famished mothers of the world." She sings pregnant with hope, bearing the Messiah, embodying the historic reversal she proclaims. Who shall mother the Messiah? Not a well-protected queen, not someone blessed with a bounteous table and a peaceful life, not a well-regarded woman of influence. Indeed, there is nothing wrong with these things; peace and abundant nourishment are among the blessings hoped for in the messianic age. But the world is dis-

torted by sin. People accumulate power and wealth at the expense of others. Suffering is rampant. And the pattern persists through the generations. Into this unjust situation comes the choice of God, Creator and Redeemer of the world. Hearing the cries of the oppressed, seeing their misery, knowing well what they are suffering, coming down to redeem, the Holy One aims to turn the unjust order of things upside down and make the world right again, being faithful to the covenant promise. In the deepest revelatory insights of Jewish and Christian traditions, there is no other God. Thus God's choice of Mary to give birth to the Messiah is typical of divine action. As Janice Capel Anderson explains, just as "God has chosen a female servant of low estate to bring the Lord into the world and exalted her, so will God overturn the proud, rich and mighty and exalt the pious, hungry, lowly." Read through these eyes, Mary's song of God's victory over the powerful becomes a song about the liberation of the most nondescript poor people on this earth. Imagine the world according to the defiant Mary's Magnificat, invites African writer Peter Daino: a heavenly banquet and all the children fed.

Through Women's Eyes

This visitation scene, with its high point in the Magnificat, garners rich attention in women's theological reflection. Once the analysis of patriarchy is in place, Mary's song of God's victory over those who dominate others rings with support for women in the struggle against male domination as well as against racism, classism, heterosexism, and all other demeaning injustice. "Mary's song is precious to women and other oppressed people," Schaberg writes, "for its vision of their concrete freedom from systemic injustice—from oppression by political rulers on their "thrones" and by the arrogant and rich." Mary preaches, she continues, as a prophet of the poor and those who are marginalized. "She represents their hope, as a woman who has suffered and been vindicated."

The Spirit who vivified Mary and empowered her prophetic voice is the same Spirit who inspires and vivifies women of all ages. Remembering her in the cloud of witnesses, women draw many and varied lessons of encouragement in her company. One of the strongest and most unusual in the light of traditional mariology is the right to say no. "Men toiling in the service of male power interests represent Mary only as the woman who knew how to say yes." Indeed, at the annunciation Mary uttered her yes to the call of God's Spirit, a consent to adventure that has been used so abominably to promote the passive submission of women. Here her *fiat* finds its home in her defiant resistance to the powers of evil. She takes on as her own the divine no to what crushes the lowly, stands up fearlessly and sings out that it will be overturned. No passivity here, but solidarity with divine outrage over the degradation of life and with the divine promise to repair the world. In the process she bursts out of the boundaries of male-defined femininity while still every inch a woman. Singing of her joy in God and God's victory over oppression, she becomes not a subjugated but a prophetic woman.

Catholic women in whose tradition Mary has been a significant figure wrestle with the significance of this canticle for their own subordinate position in current church structures. With no little irony, Gebara and Bingemer cite the homily preached by Pope John Paul II in Zapopán, Mexico, where he pointed to Mary of the Magnificat as a model for those "who do not passively accept the adverse circumstances of personal and social life and are not victims of alienation, as they say today, but who with her proclaim that God 'raises up the lowly' and, if necessary, 'overthrows the powerful from their thrones.'" If this is applied to women's struggle for full participation in governance and ministry in the church, the reversals of the Magnificat become rife with significance for ecclesial life. "How is it possible," Marie-Louise Gubler writes, "to pray Mary's song each night at Vespers without drawing spiritual and structural consequences for the church?" Indeed, Mary's prophetic speech characterizes as nothing less than *mercy* God's intervention into a patriarchal social order. Not only Mary but the women disciples in Luke, "believing sisters of Jesus' believing mother," grasp that God is no longer to be sought in the clouds, as the men of Galilee once thought, but here on earth, in the flesh, in birth, and in a grave, however surprisingly empty. God is to be sought and found in daily encounters with suffering, in tears and in the laughter of the poor, in the hungry of this earth, and in the groaning of creation. "Mary's prophetic song stands at the beginning of all this. How is it, then, that the body of the resurrected one, in the dual sense of sacrament and the church, has ended up exclusively in the hands of men?" (Mary-Louise Gubler). Susan Ross's critique spells out the implications. In many ways in the church, the mighty still occupy their thrones; the lowly still await their exaltation. "Women's very real lack of power in the church today stands as an indictment of the power structures as they exist. . . . The scandal of women's exclusion from power cannot be overlooked. Therefore any discussion of the empowerment of women must be juxtaposed with our lack of political and symbolic power and the failure of the leadership of the church to rectify this scandal." In addition to hope against their dispossessed status, women glean from this text grains of encouragement for their own creative behavior. Ruether sees in this canticle an example of a woman becoming a theological agent in her own right, actively and cooperatively figuring out the direction of the Spirit in the crisis of her time. Norris treasures Mary as an original biblical interpreter, linking her people's hope to a new historical event. In the context of hierarchal power that has silenced women's voices through the centuries, Schaberg casts Mary positively as a preacher. Noting the powerful proclamation of the good news that issues from her mouth, she writes, "Without an explicit commission to preach, she preaches as though she was commissioned," that is, with authority. In the struggle against sexism in the church, the great reversals roll on, their tone of judgment and promise resounding in the voices of prophetic women today.

It is above all in the reflections of women in the church of the poor that the profound dimensions of Mary's prophecy become clear. The Puebla Document, issued by the bishops of Latin America, describes the situation: "The poor do not lack simply material goods. They also miss, on the level of human dignity, full participation in sociopolitical life. Those found in this category are principally our indigenous people, peasants, manual laborers, marginalized urban dwellers, and in particular, the women of these social groups. The women are doubly oppressed and marginalized," not only because they are poor but because they are women in a society where machismo reigns. So described, Latin American women in base Christian communities recognize a striking analogy between their own situation and that of Miriam of Nazareth. Both dwell in poverty as a result of structural injustices in the economic order; both inhabit worlds organized around the idea of masculine superiority and the inhibition of women's gifts; indigenous women suffer added indignities due to their racial heritage and culture. Appreciation grows: Mary is one of us. This context becomes a "sound box" that amplifies the

Magnificat. Mary sings this song as a woman of the people, like millions of poor peasant women in Latin America, doubly and triply oppressed, old before their time. God regards her lowliness, as God regards theirs. Pregnant with new life, she cries out for transformation of the old order, as do they. She belongs to the tradition of women who beget their people amid suffering and despair. Who but a strong decisive woman would call down God's justice on the heads of the oppressors of the poor? Her song sets out the game plan of the coming reign of God. It reveals that women fully participate in the mission of announcing and bringing about these redemptive changes. And it keeps hope alive that poor women themselves, the least of the least, will taste justice on this earth according to the promise that God's "mercy is from age to age, on those who fear him." "Mary's song is a war chant," write Gebara and Bingemer with perhaps too much enthusiasm for a military metaphor, "God's battle song enmeshed in human history, in the struggle to establish a world of egalitarian relationships, of deep respect for each individual, in whom godhead dwells." In solidarity with her song, women on every continent find a key source for their spiritual journey and practice of the reign of God.

The multi-hued mosaic chip of the visitation scene gives us an image of Mary, reassured and applauded by another woman, speaking with prophetic authority a liberating hymn of praise. Regarding this canticle, Luther made a wise observation: "She sang it not for herself alone but for all of us, to sing it after her." Doing so places us in intense relationship to the living God, overflowing source of hope and joy, who regards the suffering world with utmost mercy and summons us together into the struggle to build a just and human world.

"And She Gave Birth"

Luke 2:1–20

THIS TESSERA SHINES with the quintessence of both bodiliness and spirituality. Mary's pregnancy ended when she gave birth, an experience that connects her with women around the world who bring forth the next generation of human beings out of their own bodies. The scene in Luke is, after the cross, the most widely recognized image in Christianity. In Bethlehem Mary gives birth to her firstborn son and lays him in a manger; angels sing the revelatory canticle announcing that this child is the Savior, Christ the Lord; shepherds visit, marvel, and return praising God; Mary ponders the meaning of it all in her heart. From much of the great art of the European Renaissance to popular commercial depictions, this birth has been bathed in a golden light commensurate with the glory of God in the angels' song. All too often it has elicited responses that range from deep to shallow sentimentality. More than any other biblical scene it has traditionally played into the ideology that sets parameters around women's lives with the dictate that their one and only God-given vocation is to be mothers. To restore this tessera to its original colors for our mosaic, we look at its elements of lowliness, bloodiness, and thoughtfulness.

Among the Poor

In Luke's story a number of elements flag the difficulty of this birth, starting with the uprootedness of its setting. Joseph of Nazareth leaves home with "Mary his betrothed," who is far along in her pregnancy. Their journey is undertaken because of a decree of the Roman emperor Caesar Augustus that all should be enrolled in their ancestral towns. Biblical scholars, finding no evidence of such an edict in Roman records that would fit the time frame of Jesus' birth, normally conclude that Luke has used an actual registration that occurred later in 6 C.E. and crafted it for his own purposive storytelling. In terms of a marian portrait, the dislocation that this trip requires becomes but the first in a series of signals that this is not a powerful family but one ranked among the lowly. The purpose of the census is to count heads for tax purposes. The Roman emperor can command tribute; the colonized villagers must hustle to obey. Thus does dominating authority ever bestride the earth, pushing around the poor of the land who have little power to change their status, unless they want to take up arms.

Far from home, these expectant parents are depicted in lowly circumstances. With "no room for them in the inn," they take shelter in a cave or stall where animals were stabled. And there "the time came for her to be delivered." In this unfamiliar, uncomfortable situation, she gave birth. It is not a great stretch of the imagination to see Mary and Joseph as transients, "equivalent to the homeless of contemporary city streets, people who lack adequate shelter," or as marginalized persons pushed to the edge, "like squatters living in the shanty towns of many big cities of the third world." In this setting, Mary, a young woman in a patriarchal society, brought her child into the world in the manner of enormously disadvantaged people, without the security of a home. She wrapped him in swaddling clothes, the traditional Palestinian way of securing a newborn, and laid him in a manger. Mentioned three times in this passage, a manger was a feeding trough for domesticated animals. It could be a movable wooden container or a low curved depression on a rocky ledge. While it served the purpose of cradling a baby, as do cardboard boxes and other such artifacts creatively appropriated by poor people today, its previous use removes any romantic pretense about the ease of this birthing scene. Meanwhile, the first to hear the message were shepherds, themselves a group of laborers of low economic and social rank, busy with their flocks. Commentators point out that the fields around Bethlehem, being relatively dry and sparsely vegetated, are "shepherd country." Proximity to Jerusalem, furthermore, might mean that shepherds worked the estates of the priests, supplying livestock for temple sacrifice. In any event, even if they owned their own flocks, shepherds were poor by definition, ranked among the lowly of Palestinian society. Hurrying with haste to Bethlehem, they "found Mary and Joseph and the baby lying in a manger." The displaced couple, the manger, and the shepherds together form a clear signal: the Messiah comes from among the lowly people of the earth.

She Gave Birth

Luke's laconic "and she gave birth" evokes a female bodily experience of profound suffering that can issue in equally profound joy. For nine months Miriam of Nazareth had been knitting her child together in her womb, sheltering a mystery of unfolding genes, developing tissues, growing movement, aiming toward viability. Now came the moment to deliver.

The risk of death in childbirth in ancient Israel, as in any pre-modern society, was very real. Its occurrence kept the average life expectancy for women to approximately thirty-five years. Whenever possible a midwife and several female helpers were on hand. According to ancient sources, the midwife brought a birthing stool that had "bars for handgrips on each side, a back to lean against, and a crescent-shaped hole cut into the seat through which the infant could pass. In the absence of a stool, the woman was to sit on the lap of another woman who was strong enough to hold her during contractions. The midwife knelt on the floor in front so that she could see both the mother's face and the emerging child." After wiping mucus from the baby's mouth and nose, allowing it to gasp its first breath, and after tying and cutting the umbilical cord, the midwife would bathe and swaddle the baby from head to toe. Then she would assist in the discharge of the mother's placenta.

Was there a midwife in the stable? How long did Miriam's labor last? With what bodily wisdom did she handle the ever-stronger contractions? When did her water break? When did she transition into the final, wrenching stage of active labor where pushing, breathing, and waves of pain fuse into an utterly concentrated moment from which there is no going back? No details are given. But the words "she gave birth" evoke that event of almost cataclysmic stress by which women bring forth new life. The phrase recalls women's pain and strength involved in laboring, sweating, counting contractions, breathing deeply, crying out, dilating, pushing hard while riven to the very center of one's being with unimaginable bursts of pain, until slowly, slowly, the baby's head finally appears and with more pushing the little creature slips from the birth canal, to be followed by the discharge of the placenta, with much bleeding, and then deep fatigue, breasts swollen with milk, and unpredictable hormonal swings. Thinking to honor Christ and his mother, later apocryphal gospels will present a picture of an effortless delivery with Jesus arriving as a ray of light or passing through Mary's womb the way the risen Christ passed marvelously through walls and locked doors (*Protoevangelium of James* 17–19). The authors assume that natural bodily processes are not worthy of the Creator, as if womb and breasts, flesh and bleeding are outside the sphere of the sacred. In the late fourth century, Ambrose would develop the theological meaning of the birth of Jesus with strange new emphasis on the physical integrity of Mary's body. As Mary T. Malone paraphrases, "Nothing of the mother was broken, changed, or altered in this birth." The utter intactness of her body, never penetrated or torn, will come to stand for the purity of the church, sealed against its enemies. Mary's virginity in childbirth will enter into church doctrine as part of her threefold virginity before, during, and after the birth of Christ, a doctrine open to multiple interpretations, as we have seen.

But Luke knows nothing of this idea. "She gave birth" has no inkling of such escape from the human condition. Later generations will honor this woman for the fact that she brought forth and nurtured the Savior; indeed, in faith language, her prophetic mothering is a charism, a gift given by God to an individual for the good of the community. For Luke this religious interpretation does not counteract the idea that Mary traveled deep into the experience common to women who bring forth a new person out of their own bodies, even at risk of their own death. Biblical scholars point out that otherwise the scene that comes next in Luke's gospel, where Mary offers sacrifice after childbirth, would make no sense. She would not need to be purified from uncleanness if this were a miraculous birth. Real blood was shed at this delivery, by a poor woman of peasant society far from home, laboring in childbirth for the first time. And it was holy.

Pondering in Her Heart

In addition to arduous physical engagement, this scene also depicts Mary intensely ruminating over the word of God. After the shepherds leave, having shared what the angels said, "Mary kept all these things, pondering them in her heart." Twelve years later she is described thinking again, after Jesus was lost and found in the temple: "his mother kept all these things in her heart" (Luke 2:51). Both of these scenes have to do with the revelation of the identity of this child. The fullness of his significance is not immediately apparent, and so Mary keeps on mulling things over. To "keep" in the sense Luke uses the word, *syntērein* and *diatērein* in Greek, means to preserve, to remember, to treasure these events. To ponder, *symballein*, means to puzzle out their meaning, to toss things together until they make sense. Experiencing things she does not fully understand, this woman turns them over in her mind, weighs them. As the ecumenical authors of *Mary in the New Testament* write, "This would mean that Mary did not grasp immediately all that she had heard but listened willingly, letting events sink into her memory and seeking to work out their meaning." No mindlessness here. She is trying to interpret her life. She is seeking to understand difficult matters concerning the lives of those she loves. She is hoping to discern how the divine Spirit is moving in their midst. She ponders in order to fathom the meaning and keep on the right path. Following Luke's image of Mary as an exemplary disciple, later generations will see here a woman at prayer, actively contemplating the word of God. Hers is a life in the process of becoming—no final answers yet available.

Fulfilling Torah

Luke 2:21–40

EVERY RELIGIOUS TRADITION observes customs surrounding the birth of a child that welcome the new life and initiate the child publicly into the community. Usually called the "presentation in the temple," Luke's next tessera depicts Mary and Joseph as religiously observant Jews who carry out these rituals after Jesus' birth according to the Law of Moses. With the Messiah now present, the text itself is focused on the manifestation of this child as "a light for revelation to the Gentiles and for glory to your people Israel," two equal dimensions of the one salvation that God has made ready. In this context, we gain a piece for our mosaic by observing how the acting subjects of the text are "the child's father and mother." Here we glimpse Mary, a young daughter of Israel, now decidedly part of a married, parenting couple, growing into the long line of mothers in Israel, celebrating her childbirth in accord with prescribed ritual.

Even though the episode roughly follows common practice, biblical scholars point out that this narrative contains several inaccuracies, such as implying that both parents need to be purified rather than just the mother, she being the only one who had bled in childbirth. This confusion is probably due to the fact that Luke, being Gentile, had a general knowledge of Judaism while being unfamiliar with the intricacies of how customs actually worked. Scholars concerned for gender equality today also raise obvious questions about the particulars of this part of the Law of Moses, such as the higher valuation of male children as seen in their consecration to God, the doubled time for purification made necessary by a female child, and the status of ritual impurity attached to a woman after childbirth. No other episode, however, better portrays Mary and Joseph of Nazareth as active parents committed to the heritage of their ancestors.

Fulfilling the Law

The scene is pervaded with an atmosphere of traditional Jewish piety, with the couple embodying the spirit of religious fidelity. After eight days they circumcise the baby, cutting the covenant into his very flesh in the tradition of Abraham. They name him Jesus. Forty days after his birth, they go up to the temple in Jerusalem to present him to God and to carry out the required ritual of purification. It is not hard to imagine them climbing the great staircase, babe in arms, emerging into the Court of the Gentiles, buying a pair of birds under the portico, heading into the Court of Women, Joseph going forward into the Court of the Israelites, Mary handing over her sacrifice to a Levite, both following the actions of the priest who kills and offers the birds, the great fire roaring on the altar. The sentiments of this young woman's prayer, expressed so clearly in her *fiat* and so powerfully in her Magnificat, find expression in this dramatic moment of ritual offering now that she has delivered her baby. Here the young friend of God called to a prophetic work, who has sung her Magnificat, given birth, and pondered the meaning of it all, carries out with her husband the law of the covenant in ceremonies imbued with their people's profound gratitude for the living God's gracious and liberating care. Depicting so clearly Mary's religious engagement in temple worship according to Torah, this text offers a strong antidote to a remembrance that would erase her Jewish identity and paint her as a Gentile Christian.

Once again these parents are portrayed as among the poor of the land. Leviticus instructs the woman to bring a first-year lamb; but "if she cannot afford a sheep, she shall take two turtledoves or two pigeons, one for a burnt offering and the other for a sin offering; and the priest shall make atonement on her behalf, and she shall be clean" (Lev. 12:8). According to these criteria, their very offering reveals their social location at the insignificant lower ranks of society. Nevertheless, two charismatic older people, emblems of maturity and wisdom, intercept their progress across the great court. Simeon, who is led by the Spirit to show up on this day, and Anna, called a "prophet," who remained always in the temple, joyfully proclaim in this sacred space of Jewish worship that salvation has come in this child. Cradling the baby in his arms, Simeon sings a canticle that praises God for allowing his old eyes to see this coming of redemption to Israel and the Gentiles; now, he prays, he is ready to die. Eighty-four-year-old Anna's response is particularly intriguing. Rather than getting ready for death, she goes to work spreading the good news. We never hear her actual preaching, but are told that she kept on praising God and "speaking about the child to all who were looking for the redemption of Jerusalem." Once again, we get a glimpse of Mary being encouraged to go on with her life's work through the ministry of a woman.

The Sword of Discernment

The tone of the scene changes suddenly as Simeon utters an ominous oracle declaring that a price will be paid. The child will be a sign of contradiction, and as for his mother, "a sword will pierce your own soul too." Soul and spirit stand for the whole self, the heart, the personal 'being' with which Mary proclaimed the greatness of the Lord. What is the meaning of the prophecy that her whole person would be run through with a sword? Long-standing popular interpretation has taken the sword to refer to the sorrow she would experience under the cross when Jesus suffered, died, and then was pierced with a lance. Part of the difficulty with this view, however, is that "there is no evidence that Luke or his community ever thought that Mary was present at Calvary." Her absence from the group who witnessed Jesus' death, burial, and empty tomb, whom Luke indicates were "Mary Magdalene, Joanna, Mary the mother of James, and the other women with them" (Luke 24:10), indicates that in this gospel the sword does not symbolize this particular suffering. Raymond Brown points out that starting with theologians in the early church numerous other meanings of the sword have been suggested, including a scandalized doubt that pervades Mary's soul during the crucifixion, or her own violent death, or she herself being rejected, or her pregnancy being illegitimate, or the fall of Jerusalem which she lived to see, or the word of God, or her enmity with the serpent from the garden in Genesis. Because they are extraneous to Luke's text, these explanations are as implausible as the popular idea that the sword stands for her sorrow at the cross. Drawing on the image of the sword in Ezekiel 14:17, where a sword of judgment passes through the land, Brown suggests that a more plausible interpretation is that for Luke this sword signifies spiritual discernment. Hearing the word of God and keeping it will not happen easily but will require struggle to arrive at wisdom. Miriam of Nazareth will be tested in the depths of her faith. As Reid writes, "What Simeon intimates is that Mary, like all disciples, will experience difficulty in understanding God's word. She was not given automatic knowledge and insight about her son and his mission." In truth, as Norris reflects, far from embodying a passive, submissive femininity, Mary wrestled with the living God as something of a biblical interpreter, hearing, believing, and pondering the word of divine promise even when it pierced her soul like a sword. This is hardly passivity, but faith, the strong faith of a peasant woman.

Blessed Together

Woven through this scene that portrays Mary fulfilling Torah and walking her journey of faith are also distinct threads of her partnership with Joseph. As Luke writes, "they" brought the child up to Jerusalem; "they" offered sacrifice; Simeon encountered "the parents" doing for Jesus what was customary under the law; "the child's father and mother" reacted with awe to his revelatory words. And in a moment little depicted in Christian art, "the child's father and mother marveled at what was said about him; and Simeon blessed them. . . ." What a striking development, the young married couple wrapped in blessing from this wise old elder, prayed over and remembered before God, together. It is not Mary alone who is blessed here, nor Joseph on his own. The two are bonded in marriage, adjusting to the care of a new baby, and divine favor is invoked upon "them" as such. Ambivalence dogs our reflection. Feminist scholars point out that according to the custom of the times, this was an arranged, patriarchal marriage and thus not something that women searching for equality would aspire to today. Furthermore, Mary is here incorporated into a patriarchal text rather than subverting it as in the annunciation and visitation stories. At the same time, in a church tradition that has long ignored Mary's married status in favor of an idealized portrait of the virgin mother and, more to the point, has used that image to relegate married women to subordinate status, it is surely liberating to give Mary back her marriage, to give her back her relationship with the man with whom she shared her life, for better or worse. And to know that this is blessed.

This episode as a whole ends with a summary statement that implies years of partnership in parenting: "When they had finished everything required by the law of the Lord, they returned to Galilee, to their own town of Nazareth. The child grew and became strong, filled with wisdom, and the favor of God was upon him." Jesus grew up not in a vacuum but in the circle of his Galilean family. It is more than likely that at least some of his understanding of God's power to save came from his Jewish parents who, during the decisive years of his growth, taught him about the compassionate, liberating God of the Hebrew scriptures.

Losing and Finding

Luke 2:41–52

IN THE FINAL SCENE of the infancy narrative, Luke brings the reader back once more to the temple in Jerusalem twelve years later. After the Passover feast Jesus remains behind, only to be found by his terribly worried parents after a three-day search. Their reunion sets the stage for the high point of the story, where Jesus declares that his primary allegiance is to God's business, to being "in my Father's house." This narrative has all the earmarks of a typical Hellenistic biographical tale in which a childhood incident foreshadows the greatness of the person in adulthood. Its point is christological, borne in the pronouncement of the deep relationship between Jesus the Jew and the God he experiences in a most intimate way. At the same time, both the language and content of the story give us another memory of Miriam of Nazareth in action. From this we glean one more tessera for our mosaic, a complex picture of parenting.

Note that this family is once again depicted as observant of Jewish tradition, traveling up to Jerusalem for the most important pilgrimage feast in the calendar. The firstborn son is now old enough to accompany them, taking another step in growing into his religious heritage. They travel in the company of "their relatives and acquaintances," a typical pilgrimage party of family members and village neighbors sharing the joyful spirit of the festival as well as giving each other safety in numbers. Their return begins "when the feast was ended," indicating they had all observed the full custom of purification, sacrificing a lamb, eating the Passover meal, and observing the days of unleavened bread that followed. One day into the return journey, disaster strikes. Anyone who has ever loved a child in danger can fill in the blanks of this narrative, which overlooks the intervening search and skips to the parents' finding the boy "after three days." Their dramatic reunion after a frantic search is again redolent of Jewish custom. They find Jesus in the temple in the midst of the teachers of the Law, "listening to them and asking them questions," while giving back answers filled with insight. This young man on the brink of adulthood has studied Torah and takes delight in debating it. Give credit to his parents.

Human Anguish

Parenting well, besides demanding an enormous amount of intelligence and energy, places the heart in a vulnerable position. Running through the joy of relationship with children in daily life and through all the milestones of their growth, there is also the background fear that harm may befall these young creatures, injuring them in ways that parents cannot prevent however responsible they may be. The joy and the suffering together are facets of love, which is expressed in the paradoxical mix of relief and anger that parents experience after danger has passed. The confrontation between Jesus and his parents in this story plays out this theme. "When his parents saw him they were astonished; and his mother said to him, 'Son, why have you treated us like this? Look, your father and I have been so worried looking for you.'" The verb Luke uses for worry, *odynasthai* in Greek, connotes severe mental pain or sadness, overwhelming anxiety. Two other scenes where Luke uses this term underscore its heaviness. In the parable of the rich man who ignores the poor man starving at his gate, both eventually die; the rich man cries out to Abraham, "have mercy on me and send Lazarus to dip the tip of his finger in water and cool my tongue, for I *am in agony* in these flames" (Luke 16:24). In Acts, Paul takes leave of the elders of the church in Ephesus; "there was much weeping among them all; they embraced Paul and kissed him, *grieving* especially because of what he had said, that they would not see him again. Then they brought him to the ship" (Acts 20:37–38). The anguish of a soul in hell, the heart-wrenching sorrow of saying a final goodbye—these are analogies for the torment felt by Mary and Joseph looking for their lost boy. It is no wonder that when they find him, her words carry an unmistakable tone of rebuke and reproach accompanying their relief. She corrects him, scolds him, complains about his behavior. Jesus' response in turn, far from being contrite, distances himself from his parents' concern. He reproaches them for searching with such anxiety. Brown points out that Jesus' answer even carries a tone of grief that his parents have understood him so poorly. Intellectually curious about matters religious and enamored of the whole temple experience, this is a village boy discovering his vocation. His calling lies in the service of God, which takes priority over family ties. The world beyond the village beckons.

When Jesus finished explaining himself to his parents, "they did not understand what he said to them." Biblical scholars warn against toning down their incomprehension. It functions in Luke as a narrative necessity because Jesus' divine sonship, while announced from his conception, becomes fully appreciated only in the christology of the post-resurrection church. Before then, scope for pondering and deciding is given to every character in the narrative. This literary reason, based in the actual course of the historical development of Christian faith, can be accompanied by existential interpretation. It is never easy to raise a child. When children are precocious, navigating the waters of parental love and responsibility becomes ever more complex, the more so as they get older. The tension and upset between parents and child in this scene are palpable. The boy went off to chart his own course. The parents did not understand—no idealization possible here.

"Your Father and I"

As in the presentation in the temple, Mary and Joseph are depicted in this story as a full-fledged married couple and parents of this son. The scene begins with their joint action: "Now his parents went to Jerusalem every year at the feast," and ends with Jesus' returning to their common home: "And he went down with them and came to Nazareth, and was obedient to them." In between, the pronoun "they" occurs eight times with the verbs that move the action: they sought him, they did not find him, they found him, they were astonished, they did not understand. In an unusual departure from patriarchal protocol, this story depicts Mary rather than her husband speaking in the name of both parents when she reprimands their son. This is odd, because overall in this infancy narrative Joseph acts as the rightful, legal, even if not actual, father of Jesus. Commentators note the likelihood that Luke received this temple story, in which Joseph appears straightforwardly as Jesus' parent, from a source that knew nothing of the annunciation story or its implied point that Joseph was not the biological father of Jesus. This literary artist lets the inconsistencies stand, just as in the coming chapters he will at one point slip in a restriction to paternity—Jesus began his ministry "being (as was supposed) the son of Joseph" (Luke 3:23)—while at the same time having the Nazareth villagers respond to the preaching of their native son by exclaiming "Is this not Joseph's son?" (Luke 4:22) with no qualifications. The point to remember is that Luke portrays Mary having a partner in parenting, at least for twelve years. Reflecting on the significance of these years, Indonesian theologian Marianne Katoppo recalls a cartoon on the wall of the World Council of Churches' editorial office in Geneva. It depicts an obviously pregnant Mary and a young Joseph, who says to her, "When you're the Mother of God, will you still be my Mary?" Underneath, the caption reads: "Do we ever think that they loved each other? 'Joseph my husband,' 'Mary my wife.' A child listens. And grows. And becomes the lover of humankind." Mary and her husband are companions in faith and married collaborators in child-raising. In this relationship, furthermore, she is no passive partner but speaks out and takes initiative, as this scene depicts. Together they create a home that nurtures life.

Thinking Mother

In this scene Jesus has reached the brink of maturity, physically and spiritually. In its aftermath he returns to the family fold in Nazareth, not to be heard from again until he starts his ministry at around the age of thirty. Once again we are told that Mary "cherished all these things in her heart." And, as Luke summarizes the years that roll by, "Jesus increased in wisdom and in stature, and in favor before God and human beings." It takes so much parenting for this to happen! It takes so much nourishing care for a newborn to negotiate the hazards of infancy and reach the second year of life. Even today, in countries with a high rate of infant mortality, the first birthday is a great cause for celebration. Each year after that brings new challenges of survival and growth, the whole marvelous panoply of a developing human being. The person or persons charged with watching over this progress are committed to long-term love in action. So much practical care, providing nourishment, cleaning up, providing clothing for a changing body; so much teaching, encouraging, disciplining; so much holding, providing intuitive psychological support, wiping away tears. So much loving. The summary statements about Jesus' growth cover over the enormous amount of mothering he received, and the fathering, without which he would not have reached adulthood physically, emotionally, and spiritually as the person he became. And through it all Mary of Nazareth kept pondering, kept thinking about the meaning of her life and the lives of those she loved, kept walking her journey of faith with God.

I want to be very careful here, since holding up Mary's motherhood as a model for all women is one of the neuralgic points in traditional mariology. Social customs surrounding the family are undergoing epochal shifts in our day. It becomes clear that not all women want to be mothers, nor need they be in order to be true women. Women who do bear children are finding ways to combine career and family with more or less satisfaction. Some men are staying home to raise their children. In wealthy societies, thanks to longer life expectancy, even women who assume traditional maternal roles will spend more years without children at home than with them. Here is where the principle that the circumstance of Mary's life provides no paradigm for all women bears critical fruit. There are many avenues along which women may rightly live out their human vocation, traditional motherhood being but one. Even if Mary is to function as an exemplar, Paul VI's teaching becomes ever more germane: she is an exemplar not in the particular social conditions of the life she led, but in the way in her own life she heard the word of God and kept it. By implication, responding to this word of God may take many creative forms in women's lives.

The question we are pursuing is the slightly different one of how to remember her in a liberating way in the midst of the community of the church. This episode presents her as a married woman and a mother, thinking, praying, full of initiatives, living out her familial relationships in Nazareth, which village summons up the peasant culture, economic stresses, and political oppression that formed the context of her hard-working life. In this time and place, year in and year out, far from temple, priesthood, and sacrificial ritual, she walked faithfully with her God. Respecting her particularity, we remember her in solidarity with women everywhere whose life energies literally mother the next generation, and with all who use their generative powers to nurture and build up healthy lives in the social and natural worlds.

Wine at the Wedding

John 2:1–11

THE SOUNDS OF FEASTING fly through the next tessera with robust joy, halt for a tense spell, then resume with even greater merriment. "There was a wedding in Cana of Galilee, and the mother of Jesus was there. Jesus with his disciples had also been invited to the wedding." Amid the feasting, dancing, and singing, unfortunately the wine gave out. When the mother of Jesus noticed and brought this to his attention, he declined to get involved for "my hour has not yet come." Disregarding his hesitation, she bid the servants to follow his word, which they did, filling to the brim six stone water jars with a capacity of twenty-plus gallons each. When the chief steward tasted the liquid it had changed into excellent wine, a point on which he complimented the groom. The text itself concludes by pointing out the significance of this extravagance: "Jesus did this, the first of his signs, in Cana of Galilee, and revealed his glory; and his disciples believed in him."

In the view of biblical scholarship, the story of the wedding feast at Cana has all the earmarks of a popular story or folktale. It originally circulated to express people's interest in the early, hidden life of Jesus, the finding of the twelve-year-old boy in the temple probably being another example. Given the existence of different types of literature in the Bible, Raymond Brown observes, "there is no reason why, alongside inspired history, one could not have inspired fiction or inspired popular narrative." Scholarly techniques determine the literary genre one is dealing with, but for any story to become scripture, whether historically based or not, it must become a vehicle of God's message of salvation. "The evangelist is not responsible for the origin or historicity of the story; he is responsible for the message it serves to vocalize." As the closing remark of the Cana narrative explains, its main purpose is christological, to reveal the person of Jesus gifted with the glory of the Messiah. Like virtually every other scene in the Gospel of John, it does this through rich use of symbolism. Both wedding feast and banquet are well-known biblical themes that symbolize the coming messianic days. Abundance of wine is also a consistent figure for the joy of the last days, promised in many prophetic utterances: "the mountains shall drip sweet wine, and all the hills shall flow with it" (Amos 9:13). In this gospel the wine, more than one hundred gallons of it, signifies the abundant gift of salvation for which light, water, and food are other Johannine symbols. The motif of Wisdom's presence in this scene also carries a christological message. In Proverbs Holy Sophia prepares a banquet, inviting people to eat of her bread and drink of her wine. The very act of drinking her wine is a symbol for accepting her message. Those who do so lay aside immaturity and find fullness of life, walking in her way of insight (Prov. 9:1–6). Here in Cana we have Jesus, already revealed in John's prologue as the incarnation of divine Wisdom, providing wine in abundance to drink and eliciting belief from the disciples.

Given this plethora of christic symbolism, it would be surprising if the figure of the mother of Jesus, never given her personal name, did not also have a symbolic function. While affirming this to be the case, scholarly opinion is deeply divided over the significance of her words and actions in this scene. She is an image of the true believer because of her faith in Jesus; no, she has good intentions but imperfect faith, seeing him only as a wonder-worker; no, she is an example of unbelief because she overrode his preferences; well, there is no reference to Christian faith here, but only a portrait of a mother with exuberant belief in the ability of her offspring. Again, Jesus' initial resistance to her request is a rebuke; it is not a rebuke but the Johannine version of the Synoptic saying that hearing the word of God and doing it are more important than physical family ties; it is neither of these but part of the typical gospel pattern of request-resistance-persistence-granting, as can be seen in the second Cana miracle, where Jesus cures the official's dying son only after being repeatedly petitioned (John 4:47–50). Again, the mother of Jesus here is a collective personality, a symbol of the church; no, she is an individual personality with an important symbolic function; no, she is an inessential figure whose function of getting the action rolling could have been filled by anyone else. Mary's presence in this scene ties Cana to the cross, the other Johannine scene in which she appears and where Jesus' hour has now come; no, the two scenes are not clearly related. Mary's function here is either so unique as mother of Jesus or universal as an ideal disciple that it offers little insight regarding women's participation in church leadership roles; to the contrary, her words and deeds offer an intriguing portrait of a woman as leader and catalyst in the mission of Jesus rife with implications for women's empowerment. Navigating my way through this exegetical minefield, I clarify once again that my purpose is not to adjudicate these disputed interpretations in the rich field of Johannine scholarship, let alone write yet another commentary on John. We are seeking answers to the question, How do we remember her? What does this Cana story, this little colored stone tile, contribute to the marian mosaic of dangerous memory being constructed here from a liberating, feminist perspective? Taking this narrative as a whole, I glue this tessera in to catch and reflect back the strong light of the two sentences attributed to the mother of Jesus at the wedding.

They Have No Wine

While highly symbolic, this story is surprisingly grounded in the historical reality of the times. About nine miles north of Nazareth, Cana was a similar small village of mostly peasant farmers struggling under Roman and Herodian rule. The wedding celebrated the second stage of marriage, when the bride traveled to her husband's home, often in a quasi-formal procession. A festive wedding supper with friends and relatives followed, sometimes lasting through the night into the next day. It is doubtful whether the full week of feasting reported of wealthy urban families could be afforded in the straitened economic circumstances of these villagers. The six stone jars "for the Jewish rites of purification" sound a further authentic note, being found today in archaeological digs in Galilee and interpreted as evidence for the Jewish character of the Galilean population. According to levitical purity laws, stone jars were to be used instead of common clay pots because the latter more easily absorbed contamination.

"They have no wine." This was more than an embarrassment to the providers of the feast and the couple whose union was being celebrated, though it was certainly that. It was a concrete, painful reminder of the precarious economic situation in which the wedding guests all lived. Acting in a decisive and confident manner, Mary named the need and took initiative to seek a solution. Because she persisted, a bountiful abundance soon flowed among the guests. Feminist reflection espies here the kind of woman whose movements typically run counter to the expectations of idealized femininity. Far from silent, she speaks; far from passive, she acts; far from receptive to the orders of the male, she goes counter to his wishes, finally bringing him along with her; far from yielding to a grievous situation, she takes charge of it, organizing matters to bring about benefit to those in need, including herself. Her words ring with the tones of prophecy, deploring and announcing hope at the same time. From this angle, she stands in solidarity with women around the world who struggle for social justice for themselves and their children, especially daughters. "They have no wine," nor security from bodily violation, nor equal access to education, health care, economic opportunity, nor political power, nor cultural respect because of their race or ethnic heritage, nor dignity due their persons as created in the image and likeness of God herself. Uttering these words, women can be empowered to turn away from socialized lack of self-esteem and docile acceptance of marginalization to engage instead in critical praxis on behalf of their own good. Every step to secure these human blessings, starting with the cry "we do not have it, we should have it," shares in God's own compassionate desire to establish the divine reign of justice on this earth.

As it works out in the churches, wherever an entrenched clerical system wielding specious arguments keeps women from the ecclesial leadership of the altar, the pulpit, and the decision-making chamber, "they have no wine" reverberates with critical hope for women's full participation in the ministries of the church. Where this restricting of women's Spirit-given gifts, as well as the gifts of men who are married to them, consequently renders whole communities deprived of the Eucharist, "they have no wine," literally no consecrated bread or cup of salvation, calls for the old water of outmoded, patriarchal practice to be transformed into renewed and fruitful sacramental life.

Reflecting with the poor in third-world contexts, theologians discover yet further profound insight in this portrait. In Brazil, Gebara and Bingemer note that in this scene Mary stands among the people, herself a member of the group without wine, and speaks the hope of the needy. And that night the poor community of Cana in Galilee "becomes the place where God's glory is made manifest as men and women drink wine, make merry, and celebrate the wedding feast." The story continues today as the figure of the mother of Jesus accompanies the poor in their ongoing struggle for bread and human rights. In view of the symbolism of the story, her words reverberate with the deep desire people feel today for their own messianic liberation. Her cry as spokeswoman from among the people energizes their hope: "They have no wine, nor peace, freedom, rights, food, housing, jobs, health. . . ." In India a similar reflection places the mother of Jesus in solidarity with people who are humiliated. Then as now, "they have no wine" resonates among the voiceless, empowering those who are marginalized "on account of economic colonialism, colour prejudice, caste distinction, racial discrimination, religious fanaticism." Extrapolating to a global context, Mary's strong impulse to call for relief corresponds to God's own dearest desire, giving us in the Cana story an enacted parable of the coming of the reign of God's hospitality. As part of the dangerous memory of the mother of Jesus, this challenging plea addresses the conscience of the body of Christ today, especially in the richest nations on earth. "They have no wine, no food, no clean drinking water": you need to act.

Do Whatever He Tells You

With these words the mother of Jesus alerts the servants to listen to his word and follow his way. In order to grasp the significance of this point, we need to step back and understand that women play surprisingly significant roles in the gospel of John as a whole, both in the number of incidents recounted and their theological consequence. Filled with the Spirit, they exhibit deeply wise knowledge of Jesus, take steps to support and encourage his mission, and act to witness his message to others. Feminist scholars credit these powerful portraits to the situation of John's church community, where women were "enabled by the communal prophetic experience which made every believer a source of spirit and life," where "leadership and structure . . . [seem] to have been dynamic and charismatic in character," and where despite struggle women exercised apostolic leadership functions (Mary Rose D'Angelo). This context in turn shaped John's robust presentation of women's ministerial actions. In addition to the Cana story, where Jesus begins his public ministry in response to the initiative of a woman, the gospel includes numerous others.

• The Samaritan woman, who enters into theological conversation at the well, whom Jesus also addresses as "Woman" and to whom he reveals his messianic identity, acts on her own initiative to bring news of this Messiah to her townspeople. Many people "believed in him because of the woman's testimony" (John 4:39), marking her as a highly successful early missionary to the Samaritans.

• Martha of Bethany, whose word summoned Jesus to the grave of her dead brother, acts as a primary spokeswoman for her community's faith. To Jesus' revelation that he is the resurrection and the life, her confession "you are the Christ, the

Son of God, the one who is coming into the world" (John 11:27) parallels that of Peter in Matthew's gospel, marking her as the leader in this gospel responsible for articulating the community's christological confession.

• Mary of Bethany, anointing Jesus' feet with costly, fragrant ointment and wiping them with her hair, flags the end of Jesus' public ministry. Her faithful love stands in sharp contrast to the betraying heart of Judas, one of the Twelve. Jesus himself discredits male objection to her ministry of anointing with the words "Leave her alone!" (John 12:7). Her deed stunningly anticipates his command to wash one another's feet as a sign of following his path of love, marking her as an exemplary disciple.

• Mary Magdalene, who stood by the cross of Jesus, was first to the tomb on Easter morning, and called Peter and the beloved disciple to witness the emptiness of the grave. Even more striking, she herself was the first among the disciples to experience an appearance of the resurrected Christ. Addressed as "Woman" by the risen Lord, her commission to preach this good news to others was carried out so powerfully, and her words "I have seen the Lord" (John 20:18) bore so unmistakably the technical formula of revelation as the basis of one's witness, that centuries later the church was still calling her *apostolorum apostola,* the "apostle of the apostles." Sandra Schneiders underscores the importance of the Mary Magdalene material in this gospel:

> It shows us quite clearly that, in at least one of the first Christian communities, a woman was regarded as the primary witness to the paschal mystery, the guarantee of the apostolic tradition. Her claim to apostleship is equal in every respect to both Peter's and Paul's, and we know

more about her exercise of her vocation than we do about most of the members of the Twelve. Unlike Peter, she was not unfaithful to Jesus during the passion, and unlike Paul, she never persecuted Christ in his members. But, like both, she saw the risen Lord, received directly from him the commission to preach the Gospel, and carried out that commission faithfully and effectively.

Elisabeth Schüssler Fiorenza sums up the result of extensive research into women in the Johannine gospel with the insight that "at crucial points of the narrative, women emerge as exemplary disciples and apostolic witnesses," and this despite the androcentric nature of the traditioning process itself.

What, then, of the mother of Jesus at Cana? "It could be that this woman too, who knows of Jesus' powers and instructs others to obey him, is to be seen as an apostolic figure," Adele Reinhartz suggests. Jesus calls her "Woman," which seems to place her on the same level as the Samaritan woman and Mary Magdalene, whom he also addressed with this appellation; her actions show that she is of the same mettle. Her instruction "Do whatever he tells you" charges the servants at the wedding to turn believingly to Jesus, and they do so on the strength of her testimony. For the original readers of this gospel in John's ecclesial community, this injunction resonated with symbolic overtones. As with every apostolic exhortation, the grounds for accepting this are not because it comes from Jesus' mother per se, but because it is given by a believing disciple. Without abandoning her relationship as mother of the Messiah, and even while exercising a mother's influence, Mary of Nazareth joins the company of her sisters the Samaritan woman, Martha of Bethany, Mary of Bethany, Mary of Magdala, and a host of other women, remembered and forgotten, as an exemplary woman disciple among other disciples, recognized by the love and apostolic witness to Christ that they give.

This tessera reflects the picture of a celebrative woman calling for more wine at the wedding, a spokeswoman of the hope of the disenfranchised and the poor, and an apostolic witness who leads others to Christ. These images are not mutually exclusive. By overlaying them we gain a powerful memory that gives impetus to women's vocation in church and world in mutuality with men living the Christian faith today in all its complexity.

Near the Cross

John 19:25–27

DEATH. IRREVERSIBLE, irrevocable, shutting down a person's time forever. Worse when it occurs as the result of an act of violence. Causing unnameable grief in the hearts of those who love and lose another. Worse when the loss occurs as the result of an act of violence. Decisively, incredibly final.

In John's gospel the scene is described in brief shorthand: "standing near the cross of Jesus were his mother, and his mother's sister, Mary the wife of Clopas, and Mary Magdalene." The dying Jesus, seeing his mother and the disciple whom he loved, addressed them both: "Woman, behold your son. . . . Behold, your mother." From that time on the beloved disciple took her into his home. Then Jesus knew that everything was finished. After crying out his thirst and sipping sour wine, "he bowed his head and gave up his spirit." He died. The subject of countless works of art, this scene conjures up all the anguish and desolation a woman could experience who had given birth to a child, loved that child, raised and taught that child, even tried to protect that child, only to have him executed in the worst imaginable way by the power of the state. It is interesting to note that the gospel never describes Mary holding the body of her dead son when he is taken down from the cross. Yet the artistic image of the *pietà* truly captures the existential tone of inexpressible sadness at the heart of this event.

As with Cana, biblical scholars question whether the scene as written is actually historical or whether its origin lies in the evangelist's symbolic imagination. Jesus' death on the cross is clearly a historical event, mentioned even by Roman and Jewish writers. Similarly, the presence of women at the cross has historical warrants. All four gospels agree that a group of women kept vigil, standing firm in the face of fear, grief, and the scattering of the male disciples. Women standing near the cross or at a distance kept the death watch, their faithfulness a sign to Jesus that not all relationships had been broken, despite his feeling of intense abandonment even by God. The names of the women differ in the different gospel accounts, but the fact that they are mentioned in every gospel eloquently strengthens the argument that their presence at the cross is historically accurate in general outline. What counts against the historicity of this particular Johannine scene of the mother and the beloved disciple are its overt symbolism along with two critical considerations. First, there is no mention in the Synoptic gospels of the mother of Jesus being among the women at the cross. Luke, who places her in Jerusalem with the community of disciples at Pentecost, would likely have named her among the Galilean women if he knew that she was present at the crucifixion. His silence indicates that she was not there. Second, the gospels stress that all the male disciples fled or scattered, which leaves little room for the continued presence of one believing, beloved male disciple. This unnamed beloved disciple, not one of the Twelve, plays a role that is utterly peculiar to John's gospel. He is the witness who guarantees the validity of the Johannine community's understanding of Jesus. Their christological views might be different from those of the petrine churches, but they were still utterly authentic, a point underscored by the way the profound faith of the beloved disciple is frequently contrasted with Peter's stumbling belief.

The symbolic theological importance of the crucifixion scene in John surfaces in the idea that at the end of his life Jesus brought into being a community in the very Spirit that flowed from him on the cross. Two great figures without a name appear, the mother of Jesus and the beloved disciple. Both were historical persons but are not named here because they are functioning as symbols of discipleship. Standing by the cross they are turned toward each other by Jesus' words and given into each other's care. Henceforth they "represent the community of true believers it is Jesus' mission to establish" (Pheme Perkins). The formula "Behold" or "Look" indicates that a revelation is to follow, such as John the Baptist's cry "Behold the Lamb of God" (John 1:36) and Pilate's statement "Behold your King" (John 19:14). Beholding each other in a new relationship, the mother of Jesus and the beloved disciple mark the birth of a new family of faith founded on the following of Jesus and his gracious God. The mother/son language indicates that, just as in the Synoptic scene with the mother and the brothers, Jesus is reinterpreting family in terms of discipleship. Many biblical scholars today also note that the symmetry of the beholding between the woman and the man signals that neither is to be elevated above the other. Both are equal partners in the family of disciples, reflecting the Johannine community as a whole where to a great extent "women and men were already on an equal level in the fold of the Good Shepherd." In a word, the mother and the beloved disciple are representative of a larger group, the church. Symbolically Jesus provides a communal context of mutual love and egalitarian regard in which they shall all live after he is gone. Regarding Mary herself, the scholars of *Mary in the New Testament* offer a counterintuitive insight: "Paradoxically, if the scene is not historical and the presence of the mother of Jesus and the beloved disciple reflects Johannine theological inventiveness, that may enhance the importance of Mary for the Johannine community." It is not likely that she would signify the fundamental vocation of the community if they did not already remember her as an exemplary disciple and apostolic witness, an insight supported by having Jesus address her once again as "Woman."

Uncovering the symbolism of the mother/beloved disciple scene in John's gospel leads to rich insight into the theological links between Jesus' death, the gift of the Spirit, and the foundation of the Christian community. In terms of our project, its legitimate designation of Mary as a precious symbolic figure also has the unfortunate effect of deleting her human reality as a historical woman with a crucified son. Even if she did not stand at the foot of the cross, even if she was still in Nazareth, which seems likely, news would have reached her. Then she joined the desolate cadre of women through the centuries who experience the terrible human condition of outliving one's child. There is no speaking this racking sorrow. It is out of the natural order of things. Worse yet, this death itself did not occur in the natural order of things but was violently inflicted, preceded by excruciating torment and carried out with public shame. One never really gets over the pain when someone you love is a victim of violence. *Mater Dolorosa* is not a theological concept or a symbolic image or an archetypal experience, but a real person who got hit one day with the terrible fact that her firstborn son was dead by state execution.

Crucifixion, a particularly cruel manner of killing, was a Roman death penalty reserved for slaves and noncitizens. It was inevitably carried out in cases where people had been involved in revolt against the empire. The notice of Jesus' crime tacked to his cross read "King of the Jews," thus placing him among the dregs of messianic hopefuls who had threatened the political power of Caesar. Thousands of others were dispatched the same way—recall Josephus's account of the crucifixion of two thousand Jewish men during the uprising after Herod's death. From the purely historical point of view, Jesus suffered and died in a broad political context of Jewish suffering and death at the hand of the Romans. Mary in this tessera is a suffering Jewish mother. Her sorrow for her dead son places her in the company of her contemporaries in Galilee and Judea whose children also fell victim to the imperial power of the empire, and in the company of their descendants through the ages, including horrifically those touched by the Christian Crusades, the Russian pogroms, and the Nazi Holocaust, whose children's lives were extinguished. Emphasizing this connectedness of the historical mother of Jesus, David Flusser observes, "She belongs to the countless Jewish mothers who lament their cruelly murdered children. . . . It would not be such a bad Mariology that did not forget these sisters of Mary in the flesh."

This particular, unappeasable pain also places her memory more broadly in solidarity with mothers of children dead by state violence everywhere, for it remains horrifically the case that the life given from women's bodies keeps on being taken away by brutality, war, and terrorism. Asian women strongly identify Mary with today's "mothers who suffer as their children are being massacred and taken as political prisoners for their actions on behalf of justice and love" (Chung Hyun Kyung). Calling on her memory, grieving mothers, wives, and daughters find strength in their bitter struggle against state repression and personal despair. Latin American women theologians speak of the "shared Calvary" women suffer with Mary in the civil wars and political repression that feed on their own children's lives. Muslim Palestinian, Bosnian, and Afghani women, mothers of criminals executed in the United States, surviving mothers of Cambodian and Rwandan genocides, the mothers and grandmothers of Argentina's Plaza de Mayo still demanding to know the fate of their disappeared loved ones—all drink from the same cup of suffering. Like them, Mary suffered the anguish of not being able to save her child from the hand of torturers and executioners. The fact that Christian imagination can picture Mary standing with desolated people under all the crosses set up in the world is due to the history of her own very real grief. This memory finds its liberating effectiveness when it empowers the church's women and men to say, STOP IT. No more killing of other people's children. No more war, brutal greed, and tyranny. This is, of course, a utopian wish, a hope for a world shaped according to God's reign which will be a world with no more sorrowing mothers. On the way to this world, the memory of Mary near the cross abides, galvanizing nonviolent action to stop the violence as the only appropriate expression of faith.

"All Filled
with the Holy Spirit"

Acts 1:14–15 and 2:1–21

WITH THIS TESSERA we arrive at the center of this book's proposal to enfold Mary into the communion of saints. For here she dwells in the post-resurrection company of Jesus' disciples gathered in the upper room to await the coming of the Spirit. They are all praying, remembering, expecting. This scene appears at the beginning of the Acts of the Apostles, which was composed by Luke as the second volume of his story of Christian origins. While "the first book" he wrote was a gospel that dealt with Jesus' words, deeds, and destiny, this sequel is a companion volume that tells the story of the church and its increasingly successful mission to the Gentiles throughout the Roman empire.

Following Jesus' ascension into heaven from the Mount of Olives, the disciples returned to the upper room in Jersualem where they were staying. The text names eleven leading men in the group, and then continues, "All these with one accord devoted themselves to prayer, together with the women and Mary the mother of Jesus, and with his brothers." Obviously a mixed group of women and men comprised of Jesus' Galilean disciples and some of his family members, "the company of persons was in all about a hundred and twenty." The tessera might end there with Mary at prayer among the followers of Jesus after Easter. She is not mentioned again by name. However, the subsequent Pentecost story opens with the words "they were all together in one place," when the sound from heaven came, and the rush of a mighty wind filled the house, and tongues as of fire "rested on each one of them." While no names are given of members of this group, biblical scholars presume that the "all" refers back to the earlier list of Jesus' disciples and family members in the upper room. Hence Mary is present when "they were all filled with the Holy Spirit and began to speak in other tongues, as the Spirit gave them utterance." As part of the community that was gathered in Jesus' name, this older Jewish woman, marked by the struggles of a hard life, receives a new outpouring of the Spirit of God and raises her voice again in inspired praise and prophecy.

There is good reason for accepting this picture of Mary enfolded into the nascent Jewish-Christian community as reliable tradition. It is highly unlikely that Luke would have cast her as such an exemplary disciple from the annunciation on, someone who heard the word of God and kept it, if the community did not remember her as part of their circle. Furthermore, since Luke does not mention her among the women at the cross, the surprise of her reappearance in the Jerusalem community after Jesus' death and resurrection indicates a historical memory that she was indeed there, at least for a time. The presence of Jesus' brothers, too, is validated by the fact that James, "the brother of the Lord," became a key leader of the church in Jerusalem. This scene is constructed with beautiful artistry. Brown points out that just as Luke begins his gospel by walking the faithful Jews Elizabeth and Zechariah, Anna and Simeon, right out of the Hebrew Scriptures to witness to Jesus the Messiah, so too he gathers three groups from the gospel and walks them into Acts to bridge Jesus' ministry and the later story of the church: Mary, who witnesses to Jesus' infancy, the Twelve who witness to his ministry, and the women who witness to his death and burial (although it should be noted that the women, too, witness to his ministry). Both of Luke's volumes begin with the startling promise that the Holy Spirit will come upon main characters in the story: Mary in the gospel, the community of disciples in Acts. When the Spirit does descend, the result is new birth that comes from God: Jesus in the gospel, the church in Acts. The literary virtuosity of this author, however, does not negate the validity of the memory reflected in his work. Historically, Mary very likely belonged to the early Jerusalem church.

To have a liberating appreciation of this mosaic tile, we must correct a popular distortion. Traditional artistic depictions of Pentecost portray the Spirit descending upon thirteen figures, one woman, Mary, surrounded by twelve male apostles. The product of an androcentric imagination that erases women and insignificant men, this picture hardly does justice to Luke's text with its one hundred twenty persons. These all must be restored to the scene. We need especially to attend to "the women" present in that upper room. They are depicted not as extras but as an integral part of the praying community in Jerusalem. Although they are not named in this passage, biblical scholars assume, reasonably enough, that they are the women mentioned in Luke's gospel account of the passion. There we read that when Jesus died on the cross, "the women who had followed him from Galilee stood at a distance and saw these things" (Luke 23:49). These women were disciples, as the technical meaning of "follow" makes clear. Their function was not that of the idle crowds "gazing at" the spectacle, but that of witnesses who "saw" what happened, as the technical meaning of "see" makes clear. Their role as witnessing disciples continued when Joseph of Arimathea wrapped Jesus' corpse in a shroud and laid it in the tomb: "the women who had come with him from Galilee followed and saw the tomb and how the body was laid" (Luke 23:55). At early dawn on Sunday morning they returned to the tomb with spices and ointments to perform a final, merciful anointing, only to find it empty. Now the legitimacy of the whole Christian message hinges on their observation and interpretation. The women disciples "play an absolutely essential role in the gospel accounts . . . the identity of Jesus' tomb with the empty tomb depends on their testimony." Two dazzling messengers relayed the news of the resurrection, whereupon the women "remembered" Jesus' words. Returning to the city, they announced their discovery "to the eleven and to all the rest." At this point Luke finally names some of the women involved in this momentous revelation: "Now it was Mary Magdalene and Joanna and Mary the mother of James and the other women with them who kept repeating this to the apostles" (Luke 24:10)—a whole cadre of female witnesses to the death, burial, and resurrection of Jesus Christ. In wrenching patriarchal fashion, the women's words seemed to the men "like an idle tale, and they did not believe them" (Luke 24:11). The term for idle tale, *lēros* in Greek, "could scarcely be more condescending," forming the root of the English word delirious. It was as if the women were spouting nonsense, so much delirious humbug. Peter even ran to the tomb and saw that it was empty as the women had said; but he went home "wondering" what was going on, rather than believing in the risen Christ on the strength of the women's testimony—a not unfamiliar scene even today.

When the leader of a messianic movement dies, the movement frequently dies too. In the case of Christianity, however, something happened that changed this local Jewish movement into a worldwide religion. Many factors contributed to this development, but, as Jewish scholar Tal Ilan observes, "the initial momentum seems to have begun with the people who interpreted the events following Jesus' death as a resurrection. The gospels unanimously agree that these people were women." They saw angels where the men saw nothing. Consequently, women were not only extremely instrumental at the most critical moment of Christian history, but the basic creed of Christianity, namely, that after his death Jesus was raised to life, was initiated by women's testimony. They were the first to understand the resurrection faith that is the foundation of the church. Earlier in his gospel, Luke had depicted some of these same women traveling with Jesus around Galilee, including Mary Magdalene and Joanna, the wife of Chuza who was Herod's steward, along with Susanna "and many others" (Luke 8:2–3). This group of women disciples constitutes a moving line of continuity, from Galilee to the cross to the full tomb and the empty tomb and now to the upper room at Pentecost. All this history of these women's vocational choice in response to Jesus, their experiences of following, their brave fidelity, their outspoken witness, and men's rejection of their word, is present in that upper room. Now they are filled with "power from on high" and emboldened to speak out with more power than ever.

The gender inclusiveness of the gift of the Spirit comes to the fore when Peter speaks out to explain Pentecost to the gathering crowd. He quotes the prophet Joel:

> And in the last days it shall be, God declares,
> that I will pour out my Spirit upon all flesh,
> and your sons and daughters shall prophesy,
> and your young men shall see visions,
> and your old men shall dream dreams.
> Even upon my slaves, both men and women,
> in those days I will pour out my Spirit;

and they shall prophesy. (Joel 2:28–29,
cited in Acts 2:17–18)

Feminist insight would expand Joel to include young women having visions and old women dreaming dreams as well. The point is that a sign of messianic times occurs when not only men but women receive the Spirit; when not only free persons but slaves, even slave women who rank at the lowest rung of the social ladder, pour forth prophetic speech in the power of the Spirit given to them in like measure. This scene, key to the birth of the church, dramatically sounds the opening bell: it has begun. Witnessing to Christ, bearing Christ forward in history, the church is the creation of the Spirit firing up the hearts and loosening up the tongues of even the most insignificant person, moving the whole community to speak and act on behalf of the reign of God. It is interesting to note that this is not the only time the Spirit is given. Later on, in the shock of the first persecution, the early community prayed for courage; "and when they had prayed, the place in which they were gathered together was shaken; and they were all filled with the Holy Spirit and spoke the word of God with boldness" (Acts 4:31).

The text of Acts is a site of conflict. Given this Pentecost beginning, one would expect many stories to follow of women's leadership in preaching and prophesying. Such is not the case. Luke focuses instead on the deeds of Peter and Paul with little regard for women's ministry. Even where women are mentioned, incidentally and sporadically, as building up the church, we never hear them speak. Virtually every woman biblical scholar who deals with Acts makes the same point: the author selected his stories with androcentric interest. Desiring to impress his readers in the Roman empire with the trustworthiness of this new movement, he consistently depicted men in public leadership roles and, in order to conform with the empire's standards, kept women decorously under control in supportive positions. Having eyes mainly for elite men, he fudged women into an insignificant background ignoring the leadership roles they in fact held. "Luke is above all a gentleman's gentleman, and Acts is his book," is the telling judgment of Gail O'Day, echoed throughout women's exegesis. Consequently, Acts does not contain a representative picture of church leadership in the early decades. It tells only part of the story.

To reconstitute a fuller history, feminist scholars look to a broader spectrum of texts. They read the story of women's discipleship and apostolic witness across the canonical gospels, as we saw in the tessera of John's account of the cross. They take account of the letters of Paul, whose salutations give a vibrant picture of women's extensive participation in ministry, one that stands in contrast to women's marginalization in Acts. Recall Paul's salutation to the deacon Phoebe, leader of the church of Cenchreae; and to Junia, outstanding among the apostles in Rome; and to the wife and husband team Prisca and Aquila, leaders of a house church in Rome; and to beloved Persis, who "worked hard in the Lord" for the same community, working hard being a code phrase for leadership (see Rom. 16:1–16). They also consult second- and third-century apocryphal gospels, which take figures from Jesus' ministry and place them in situations reflective of the later church. One telling incident occurs in the apocryphal *Gospel according to Mary*. The scene opens with Mary Magdalene encouraging the disheartened, terrified male disciples by preaching to them what the risen Lord had taught her. In anger Peter interrupts asking, "Did he really speak privately with a woman and not openly to us? Are we to turn about and all listen to her? Did he prefer her to us?" Troubled at this disparagement of her witness and faithful relationship to Christ, Mary responds, "My brother Peter, what do you think? Do you think I thought this up by myself in my heart, or that I am lying about the Savior?" At this point Levi breaks in to mediate the dispute: "Peter, you have always been hot-tempered. Now I see you contending against the woman like the adversaries. But if the Savior made her worthy, who are you, indeed, to reject her? Surely the Lord knew her very well. That is why he loved her more than us." The story ends with the apostles gaining courage from Mary Magdalene's testimony and going forth to preach. Acting like detectives, scholars piece together these bits of evidence to understand that this incident reflects the second- and third-century conflict over women's ministry as an ascendant male leadership tried to suppress them. Slowly such scholarship is restoring the historical picture of women's leadership in the early church and the ensuing struggle to defeat it.

I have not forgotten Mary the mother of Jesus. But the Christian tradition of art and liturgy has forgotten the Galilean Jewish women with her who were all filled with the Spirit at Pentecost and were moved to invaluable and authoritative ministerial commitments. Reducing them to only glancing significance while focusing on the glories of Mary has robbed the whole church of the full story of its founding and deprived women of their heritage of female leadership in the Spirit. It also lies at the root of the damage androcentric mariology has done to women's spirituality and equal participation in ministry in the church. Here at Pentecost, both historically and in the text of Acts, Mary lives among the women founders of the church as well as the men. She is the mother of Jesus, who gave birth to him in troubling circumstances, taught and nurtured him, and let him go to his destiny with very great love. Other women there, Mary Magdalene,

Joanna, Mary the mother of James, and many unnamed others, are Jesus' friends and disciples who supported his ministry, witnessed his death and burial, and bore the earth-shattering responsibility of being chief witnesses to his resurrection whether the men believed them or not. Each woman brings her own history of relationship to Jesus. None is reducible to the other. With their particular gifts and history, all are vital in different ways. Their believing discipleship and varied leadership roles form a constitutive part of the apostolic church. Mary cannot be separated from the rest of this community. They are all essential to one another. This text does not portray Mary at the center of the community, as mother of the group, or as the one and only ideal member. Nor does it allow her presence to overshadow the distinctive witness and ministry of the other women. Rather, it positions her amid the community as one unique member among other unique members, the whole group living by the power and presence of the Spirit and seeking to bring that warmth and light to the world.

Mary's presence in the Jerusalem community allows for some imaginative questions. What was the conversation like between her and Miriam of Magdala, leading witness of the risen Christ? What stories did she swap with Joanna, who followed Jesus despite having wealth and social prestige to spare? What memories, hopes, and strategies did she share with the other women in this community? Perhaps she lived peaceably as a beloved old woman revered as the mother of the Messiah. Perhaps during the breaking of the bread, when listening to the women and men around the table ponder the meaning of her son's life, death, and resurrection, she shared her own wisdom, such as it was. Perhaps, too, she was an outspoken elder, weighing in with creative opinions about the incipient problems with the Gentiles and supporting the leadership in the community of women such as Mary Magdalene. She may have been concerned about the destitute among them, especially the widows; or caught by the inevitable sadness that never quite goes away after violence; or full of proclamations about what God was doing to set right the world; or encouraging the creative efforts of the young; or on fire with the Spirit in a mystic's old age. All of these scenarios are seriously imaginable.

This final tessera allows us to remember that the life of the historical woman Miriam of Nazareth was indeed a journey of faith, with significance for people struggling to negotiate the challenges of faith today. From her peasant domicile in Nazareth to the house church in Jerusalem, both of which labored to survive under oppressive economic and political circumstances; from youth to marriage to widowhood; from the birth of her firstborn to his horrendous death to hearing him proclaimed Lord, Messiah, and Savior—she walked her life's path keeping faith with her gracious God, the Holy One of Israel. Now she is an older woman wise in the Spirit. All her years of suffering and joy, danger and risk-taking, questioning and pondering, anxiety and hope, hard work and sabbath rest, intimate relationships and losses, coalesce in a new quickening. Inconceivable though it may be, the God of Israel in whom she believed has acted to fulfill the ancient promise made to her people. All creation is headed for a vivifying transformation. Death does not have the last word. "Afire with some unnamed energy," she like "all of them" is empowered to witness with boldness, bequeathing a legacy still capable of igniting hearts with hope in the living God in the midst of a world of suffering.

On the Shoulders of Giants

A Brief Bibliographic Essay

THIS BOOK DRAWS on the research of a multitude of scholars in the biblical field. Certain books, opened on my desk or floor, provided me with insight all the way through. I am indebted to *The Women's Bible Commentary*, edited by Carol Newsom and Sharon Ringe, particularly the essays by Amy-Jill Levine (Matthew), Mary Ann Tolbert (Mark), Jane Schaberg (Luke), Gail O'Day (John, Acts), and Carol Meyers on women's everyday life in biblical times. Similarly, *Searching the Scriptures*, edited by Elisabeth Schüssler Fiorenza, led me to women's wisdom about the biblical text, especially its essays by Elaine Wainwright (Matthew), Joanna Dewey (Mark), Turid Karlsen Seim (Luke), Adele Reinhartz (John), and Clarice Martin (Acts). In *Mary, Woman of Nazareth*, edited by Doris Donnelly, the essays by Donald Senior (Synoptics), Richard Sklba ('Anawim), and Pheme Perkins (John) directed my attention with sharp, significant judgments. The ecumenical volume *Mary in the New Testament*, edited by Raymond E. Brown, Karl Donfried et al., began my reflections on the historical Mary many years ago and was an invaluable companion to my writing.

In addition to these collections, other individually authored books led me to significant insights. I wore out the spine on Raymond Brown's *The Birth of the Messiah* and Jane

Schaberg's _The Illegitimacy of Jesus_. Special mention should also be made of in-depth studies of single gospels, including Joan Mitchell, _Beyond Fear and Silence: A Feminist-Literary Reading of Mark_; Elaine Wainwright, _Shall We Look for Another? A Feminist Rereading of the Matthean Jesus;_ Barbara Reid, _Choosing the Better Part? Women in the Gospel of Luke;_ Sandra Schneiders, _Written That You May Believe: Encountering Jesus in the Fourth Gospel_; Raymond Brown's commentary on the gospel of John; and Mary Rose D'Angelo's essays on all four gospels in _Women and Christian Origins_, edited by D'Angelo and Ross Kraemer.

Beyond the North American academic mainstream, I learned much from the wealth of ideas emerging from developing countries. Ivone Gebara and Maria Clara Bingemer's work in _Mary, Mother of God, Mother of the Poor_, the first full-length study of Latin American women's marian theology, gave me an entirely new angle of vision. Voices from Asia came into my study in Chung Hyun Kyung's _Struggle to Be the Sun Again_ and Tissa Balasuriya's _Mary and Human Liberation_; and from Africa in Peter Daino's _Mary, Mother of Sorrows, Mother of Defiance_. Ursula King's edited volume, _Feminist Theology from the Third World_, opened doors to insights from all continents.

Poets, too, captured my imagination and guided the way I read some texts. Kathleen Norris's _Meditations on Mary_, along with Anne Johnson's variations on the Magnificat and her prose poem _Miryam of Nazareth: Woman of Strength & Wisdom_, add the note of beauty to this study.

The community of hard-working scholars whose work I quote here is large and varied. All citations are given in full in _Truly Our Sister_ from which this book is excerpted word for word. Here is the list of sisters and brothers whose research shaped the way I presented this biblical mosaic of Mary. As a systematic theologian, I stand on the shoulders of giants.

- Carol Adams
- Ambrose
- William Arnal
- J. P. Audet
- Horst Balz
- Ana María Bidegaín
- Leonardo Boff
- Vincent Branick
- Raymond E. Brown
- John Calvin
- Chung Hyun Kyung
- Carsten Colpe
- Michael Crosby
- Mary Rose D'Angelo
- Consuelo del Prado
- Joanna Dewey
- Doris Donnelly
- Julia Esquivel
- Joseph A. Fitzmyer
- David Flusser
- Gerhard Friedrich
- Ivone Gebara
- Vernon Gregson
- Marie-Louise Gubler
- Catharina Halkes
- John Haught
- E. Hennecke
- Richard A. Horsley
- Kathleen Hurty
- Irenaeus
- Juan Alfaro
- Janice Capel Anderson
- Nehama Aschkenasy
- Tissa Balasuriya
- Schalom Ben-Chorin
- María Clara Bingemer
- Dietrich Bonhoeffer
- David Brooks
- Mary Callaway
- Judith Christ
- Raymond Collins
- Shawn Copeland
- Peter Daino
- Gerhard Delling
- Michel Desjardins
- Richard Dillon
- Michael Downey
- J. Cheryl Exum
- Donal Flanagan
- Marie Fortune
- Beverly Roberts Gaventa
- Charles Homer Giblin
- Alois Grillmeier
- Gustavo Gutiérrez
- Van Austin Harvey
- Diana Hayes
- Mary Catherine Hilkert
- B. Hubbard
- Tal Ilan
- Katherine Ludwig Jansen

- Anne Johnson
- Marianne Katoppo
- Karen King
- Hisako Kinukawa
- Ingrid Kitzberger
- Paul Krugman
- Justin Lang
- Amy-Jill Levine
- William Loewe
- Mary T. Malone
- Clarice Martin
- Daphne Merkin
- Joan Mitchell
- Dom Sebastian Moore
- Nel Noddings
- Gail O'Day
- Pheme Perkins
- Judith Plaskow
- Ignace de la Potterie
- R. J. Raja
- Barbara Reid
- Cynthia Rigby
- Susan Ross
- Sara Ruddick
- Valerie Saiving
- E. P. Sanders
- Edward Schillebeeckx
- Gerhard Schneider
- Luise Schottroff
- Donald Senior
- Richard Sklba
- Elizabeth Cady Stanton
- Elsa Tamez
- Luke Timothy Johnson
- Beverly Mayne Kienzle
- Ursula King
- Gerhard Kittel
- Ross Shepard Kraemer
- Hans Küng
- René Laurentin
- Judith Lieu
- Martin Luther
- Mary John Mananzan
- Megan McKenna
- M. Miguens
- Jürgen Moltmann
- Carol Newsom
- Kathleen Norris
- Jaroslav Pelikan
- Tina Pippin
- John Pobee
- Hugo Rahner
- Joseph Ratzinger
- Adele Reinhartz
- Sharon Ringe
- Rosemary Radford Ruether
- Letty Russell
- Katharine Doob Sakenfeld
- Jane Schaberg
- W. Schneemelcher
- Sandra Schneiders
- Elisabeth Schüssler Fiorenza
- Turid Karlsen Seim
- Dorothee Soelle
- Klemens Stock
- Samuel Terrien

- Anne Thurston
- Phyllis Trible
- Walter Vogels
- Elaine Wainwright
- Pamela J. Walker
- Manfred Weber
- Amy Wordelman

- Mary Ann Tolbert
- Sojourner Truth
- Frans Jozef von Beeck
- Barbel von
  Wartenberg-Potter
- Renita Weems

ELIZABETH A. JOHNSON is Distinguished Professor of Theology at Fordham University, a past president of the Catholic Theological Society of America, and a recipient of a Grawemeyer Award in Religion (1993) and an American Academy of Religion Award for Excellence in the Study of Religion (1999). She is the author of *Consider Jesus; She Who Is; Women, Earth, and Creator Spirit; Friends of God and Prophets;* and *Truly Our Sister.* She is also the editor of *The Church Women Want.*